Outrageous GRACE EVERY DAY

Mary DeMuth

HARVEST HOUSE PUBLISHERS
EUGENE, OREGON

Cover design by Emily Weigel Design

Cover photo © SimpleThingsHere / Shutterstock

Mary E. DeMuth is represented by David Van Diest from the Van Diest Literary Agency, 34947 SE Brooks Road, Boring, OR 97009.

Outrageous Grace Every Day
Copyright © 2019 by Mary DeMuth
Published by Harvest House Publishers
Eugene, Oregon 97408
www.harvesthousepublishers.com

ISBN 978-0-7369-7649-7 (pbk.)
ISBN 978-0-7369-7650-3 (eBook)

Library of Congress Cataloging-in-Publication Data

Names: DeMuth, Mary E., author.
Title: Outrageous grace every day / Mary E. DeMuth.
Description: Eugene : Harvest House Publishers, 2019.
Identifiers: LCCN 2019015143 (print) | ISBN 9780736976497 (pbk.)
Subjects: LCSH: Bible. Romans--Devotional literature.
Classification: LCC BS2665.54 .D46 2019 (print) | LCC BS2665.54 (ebook) |
    DDC 242/.5--dc23
LC record available at https://lccn.loc.gov/2019015143
LC ebook record available at https://lccn.loc.gov/2019981441

Printed in the United States of America

19 20 21 22 23 24 25 26 27 / VP-GL / 10 9 8 7 6 5 4 3 2 1

*To my steady, encouraging, grace-infused
mastermind group.
You have girded my resolve,
lifted me from publishing despair,
and encouraged me to live well the message of this book.*

*Thank you, Thomas Umstattd Jr., Susan May Warren,
Tracy Higley, Lacy Williams, Jim Rubart, Randy
Ingermanson, and Tricia Goyer.
I love you all.
I'm indebted to you.
And I pray for you often.*

Before You Start This
Transformational Journey…

I must admit: I have been scared to start this book. Though I've done plenty of preparation and praying, I am one of those souls quite intimidated by the book of Romans. It's thick and rich and long and multilayered. Who am I to shepherd you through it?

What I can say is this: I am a worshipper of the God who tenaciously pursued me—a sin-scarred child rescued by the life, death, and resurrection of Jesus Christ and a grateful recipient of the hope the Holy Spirit has given me.

While I consulted scholars and commentaries aplenty to better understand the nuances and intent of Paul's letter to the Romans, I first did something different. While praying about the writing, I sensed God asking me to read the entire book of Romans, all sixteen chapters, every day for three months. One day of reading for every day of this devotional. In that repetitive immersion, themes began to appear. I started feeling the rhythm of Paul's words and immersed myself in the grand story he recounted.

Romans is a long summary of the entire story of God—how he began the world, chose and delivered a people, then sent his Son so the entire world could be likewise chosen and delivered. It's a narrative of good versus evil. So much of the language within its pages is that of the law court—a judicial pardoning of sinners. It's a beautiful apologetic on the existence of God, and it's a cautionary tale for all of us who would rather live on our own terms rather than surrendering to the One who made us. There is an agonizing longing in Paul's heartbeat—his sincere desire to see the entire world come to terms with Jesus, the One who transformed him from church persecutor to planter.

This is a love story, of the Savior who leaves the ninety-nine and pursues the reckless one, of the design all along of God's redemptive plan for humanity. All this sounds ethereal, but it's actually down-to-earth. This theology has feet. And if you linger in these pages every day for three months, your walk will be changed. Not by my words, but by Scripture's.

Immersing myself in Romans for 90 days has settled my heart. I know Jesus made me right (justified) before God the Father. There's nothing I can do to alter the reality of what he accomplished on the cross. For someone who has perennially felt insecure, this is yet another aspect of the Good News—our security cannot be based on our feelings, our failures, or our family of origin. No, our security is based on the faithfulness of our Father. And we show our gratitude not by working tirelessly in our own strength with fear as our faulty motivation. No, we respond by having simple belief, in trusting that Jesus accomplished everything on the cross. His "It is finished" is the truth, and there's nothing we can do to earn anything more.

That grace, dear one, is settled. It is bedrock. We cannot shake it. It cannot dissipate.

In my three-month journey, I also had to remind myself that Paul didn't write this book to me or any other person. No, his was a letter to a group of people who gathered together to worship Jesus. So ingrained am I in American individualism that I'm prone to forget the powerful truth that we are the Body of Christ—all of us. It's not me; it's us. And we grow best alongside one another. We experience Jesus together through the varied gifts he has given us. So here's a challenge for you. Don't just pick up this devotional and read it by yourself. Grab a few friends and read it concurrently, then discuss what you've learned every week or so. You'll double your interaction with the text and cement the beautiful truths to your soul in a way that isolated reading can't.

You're about to embark on an adventure through this wide-reaching book of the Bible—one whose tendrils weave through the Old Testament and into the New Covenant. You will encounter Paul's bedrock theology, a robust view of the otherness of God, and a settled peace for your place in his ever-expanding kingdom. As an adopted child of God, you have an important part to play in the story of God that is both now and not yet.

Because of all that Good News, this will also be a worship journey. Even before I started writing this book, I sensed God calling me back to worship, to poetry set to words. So before we begin studying every chapter of Romans, you'll see a worship song I penned—an ode to the One who set me free and set my feet to dancing. I pray each song blesses you.

Oh dear one, you are loved. So very loved. And your God has gone to hell and back to secure that hope for you. If your trust muscle has atrophied amidst the pain and heartache of life, take this journey with me, walking through the book of Romans day by day for the next three months. And dare to do so with anticipation for what God will do in your heart. Dare to hope. As Paul writes, "Hope does not disappoint, because the love of God has been poured out within our hearts through the Holy Spirit who was given to us" (Romans 5:5 NASB). You are not abandoned. He lives within. And living in light of his love changes everything.

Let's begin.

ROMANS 1

When I read this chapter, I can't help but long to get clean before the Almighty God. He is everything to me, and I love and need his cleansing forgiveness.

FORGIVE ME

Lord, I've traded your glory for mine
Ignoring your nature divine
I've chased the opinions of man
I'm my own clamoring fan
Oh Lord, please forgive me

CHORUS

Forgive me
For preferring my will to your ways
Forgive me
For reveling in selfish displays
I surrender afresh
More of you; I'll be less
Oh dear Lord, please forgive me

I've been greedy for unrighteous gain
Grabbing trinkets and bits of my fame
Lord, I worked for the treasure
Heralding poverty, not pleasure
Oh Lord, please forgive me

BRIDGE

Let me boast all the more
Of your beautiful power
Let me shout all your worth
My formidable tower
You are God ever high
Yet forgiven, I rise
Oh Lord, please forgive me

Day 1

Read Romans 1:1-2

*This letter is from Paul, a slave of Christ Jesus, chosen by God
to be an apostle and sent out to preach his Good News.
God promised this Good News long ago through
his prophets in the holy Scriptures.*

ROMANS 1:1-2

Today it's hard to wrap our minds around slavery as a metaphor for our relationship with Jesus. But *slave* in this passage, *doulos* in the Greek, means exactly what you think it means: an indentured servant with few or no personal rights, signifying a relationship of servitude to a master.

But aren't we set free by Jesus's beautiful act of emancipation through the cross? In John 15:15, Jesus says he no longer calls us slaves (same word, *doulos*), but refers to us as friends. Amazing! Jesus's death and resurrection set us free to be his friends. But we, like bond servants who willingly indenture themselves to their master after emancipation, now have the freedom to exclusively serve Jesus (see Deuteronomy 15:12-17). We no longer serve ourselves, nor are we enslaved to the fleeting opinions of others. We serve Jesus only, joyfully obeying his voice because we can't bear *not* to.

Not only are we set-free slaves, but God has specifically chosen us. We are his. We are not free agents—untethered and aimless. No, we are all these things: friend, slave, an adopted child. We are wanted. Created. Sacrificed for. Loved.

In light of all that audacity, God entrusts us with a new mandate: to share the Good News (the gospel) of Jesus Christ wherever we go. Our lives are now a Christlike fragrance, infusing this broken world through the position and purpose we've uncovered. Paul reminds us in 2 Corinthians 2:16, "To those who are perishing, we are a dreadful smell of death and doom. But to those who are being saved, we are a life-giving perfume. And who is adequate for such a task as this?" You may not feel like an adequate *doulos*, but really, you are perfume—and perfume emits. It can't help but permeate, and that is now the reality of our lives—we woo others toward Jesus because he has infused us with this paradoxical perfume of freedom.

Go forth, dear slave, and permeate this broken world with Jesus, knowing that you were once enslaved to all sorts of sins and lusts and destructive living. We'll see this powerful before-and-after at work throughout the book of Romans—what we once were (held hostage by sin, producing all sorts of death) and who we now are (sacrificed for, loved, and adopted children of the God of the universe) and how we are to live (in newness of life through the power of the Holy Spirit, who lives audaciously within us). Romans is a book of hope, friend— a book that reminds us that nothing can separate us from God's powerful, sin-forgiving love. Pray along with me that your heart would be deeply encouraged, challenged, and changed by the Good News within its pages.

> *Father, thank you that you've set me free from slavery to sin and given me the privilege of being a* doulos *in your kingdom, one who serves you with absolute joy and gratitude. Would you take me on a spiritual journey through the book of Romans? Keep my heart open to all the growth you want to inaugurate in me. I am your willing, attentive servant. Amen.*

Day 2

Read Romans 1:3-7

*Through Christ, God has given us the privilege and
authority as apostles to tell Gentiles everywhere what
God has done for them, so that they will believe
and obey him, bringing glory to his name.*

ROMANS 1:5

Half the joy of experiencing a sought-after vacation is the anticipation of it. We peruse pictures of the new-to-us locale, ask questions of friends who have already adventured there, and dream alongside our family as we wait together.

In Genesis, we see God giving Abram this kind of anticipatory prelude. He's told that one day the whole earth will be blessed by his offspring (12:1-3). It's a foretaste of what would unfold—a holy teasing of the Good News. And God's not-so-subtle hinting didn't stop with Abraham. No, he continued to woo the nation of Israel through forefathers, judges, kings, and prophets—pointing to the day when his Son would change everything for everyone. In Matthew 5:17, Jesus confirms he is the fulfillment of all God's promises: "Don't misunderstand why I have come," he said. "I did not come to abolish the law of Moses or the writings of the prophets. No, I came to accomplish their purpose." Later in Matthew, Jesus explains, "I tell you the truth, many prophets and righteous people longed to see what you see, but they didn't see it. And they longed to hear what you hear, but they didn't hear it" (13:17).

Jesus arrived into our sin-darkened world wrapped in the swaddling clothes of prophetic utterances and holy Scriptures—two staples of the Jewish spiritual wardrobe. And yet they missed him. Jesus told them, "You search the Scriptures because you think that in them you have eternal life; it is these that testify about Me; and you are unwilling to come to Me so that you may have life" (John 5:39-40 NASB). It would be like planning your dream vacation to Fiji only to content yourself with holding your tickets, thinking that is all there is to the experience. Today, revel in the beauty of God's Old Testament wooing while embracing the One who brings grace and peace.

This grace and peace Paul talks about here are not fleeting; they are permanent truth—all secured through the plan of God through Jesus Christ. That is the essence of the gospel. May you grow more and more in your knowledge of his calling and your position as a well loved child of God who daily experiences needed grace and the peace that surpasses the world's understanding.

Father, help me live in anticipation of gospel transformation. I want to better understand your ever-unfolding plan from ancient epochs until now. Thank you for sending your Son to die for this broken world. Thank you for securing grace and peace for me, for everyone. Thank you for loving me. Help me spend my day worshipping you for all you have done. Amen.

Day 3

Read Romans 1:8-12

*Let me say first that I thank my God through Jesus Christ for all
of you, because your faith in him is being talked about all over
the world. God knows how often I pray for you. Day and night
I bring you and your needs in prayer to God, whom I serve with
all my heart by spreading the Good News about his Son.*

ROMANS 1:8-9

Here we see the heart of Paul toward the people he's addressing in his letter—the Jewish and Gentile believers in Rome. The word *first* here is the Greek word *proton*, which means taking a primary role. We must first thank God—not only for the people he's surrounded us with, but also for our lives, the air we breathe, and even the difficulties we face. The word *thank* has a common ring to it: *eucharisteo*—a word that means grateful. It's where we get the term *Eucharist*, which Jesus inaugurates in the last supper, where he gives thanks for the bread and wine—powerful reminders of his body and blood and essential elements of the New Covenant. This particular rendering of *eucharisteo* is present tense, which means we, like Paul, are to offer gratitude continually—all day long.

Paul transitions from gratitude to prayer, which is a powerful pattern for us to follow. We praise God for what he is doing in our midst, then we entreat him, asking him to intervene in the lives of our friends and family members. This type of prayer is similar to the kind the seventeenth-century monk Brother Lawrence practiced—a moment-by-moment interaction with God throughout the day. He wrote, "There is not in the world a kind of life more sweet and delightful than that of a continual conversation with GOD. Those only can comprehend it who practice and experience it."[1] This is the kind of prayer that changes the landscape of our inner world, and Paul practiced it often.

Paul's heart for the believers in Rome is an expanded presence. Yes, he connects with them through prayer, and he reaches them with the written word, but he longs to see them in person. You can hear his pastoral heart in these words—the longing he has to be mutually encouraged. He knows that we grow best in community, not isolation, and he demonstrates a reciprocal humility here. He is not merely a teacher, but a student who anticipates receiving from them.

May all these verses inform your day, infusing it with a holy rhythm. Make it your first jump-out-of-bed choice to worship God, then continue your dialogue with him about what worries you, particularly those people he's entrusted to your care. Then connect with others, being open to the Holy Spirit's encouragement in the two-way street of receiving and giving. Perhaps today is the day you send a card to an ailing loved one, or take the hand of a stranger and pray for a pressing need, or simply step away from the demands of life to tell God you love him.

Father, I want to worship you first. I want to spend my life thanking you, talking with you, hearing from you. Remind me today not merely to think about my own needs, but to offer prayer for others who need your intervention. Intersect my life with those who need to know that you love them. I choose to obey any promptings you give. I love you. Amen.

Day 4

Read Romans 1:13-15

*I have a great sense of obligation to people in both the
civilized world and the rest of the world, to the educated
and uneducated alike. So I am eager to come to you
in Rome, too, to preach the Good News.*

ROMANS 1:14-15

The audience for this letter is Roman Christ followers. Rome was
a powerful capital city, more than a million strong, beset with
an extreme gap between rich and poor. And if people chose the way
of Christ, they'd further alienate themselves from economic opportunity. These people suffered for their faith, so they must've longed to
have Paul visit them. He, too, hoped to see them, but because of his
insatiable desire to see Christ proclaimed everywhere—coupled with
God's insistent guidance—he stayed back to share the gospel with as
many cities and nations as he could. Chuck Swindoll calls Paul "the
chief ambassador of the good news to the world between Jerusalem
and Rome."[2] But now? Lord willing, he would make his way to them,
eagerly.

The readiness of Paul inspires us. Later, in his letter to the Ephesian church, he instructs, "As shoes for your feet, having put on the
readiness given by the gospel of peace" (6:15 ESV). This longing to see
all people meet Jesus, to be transformed by the power of the resurrection, must compel us to live our lives differently—not merely for our
own interests, but for the interests of others (Philippians 2:4). And the

ultimate interest of others, though they may not realize it at the time, is a connected, vital relationship with Jesus Christ.

What's beautiful about Paul's ambition to preach Christ is its democratic way—justification for all people. Not simply for those who could further his agenda, not merely for those with political power, not just for the popular crowd, but for everyone. We live in a world that praises the shiny, the powerful, and the celebrity. We naively think that if we can "win" someone with power, then the kingdom of God will expand exponentially, seeing one elevated human as the linchpin for church growth. But remember: God uses the weak to shame the wise (1 Corinthians 1:27-29). His kingdom is powerfully paradoxical. While on earth, Jesus chose unlearned men and several women to advance his kingdom. And the smallest, seemingly most insignificant person may become like Paul—an ambassador to all.

Later we'll see in Romans 12 just how egalitarian Paul is. He advises us to love all people—the educated, the civilized, the uneducated, the uncivilized, those of high and low reputation. The Good News is for all people, and it's our privilege to share it with everyone, not merely the people we identify with the most, not only the outcasts, and not for the sake of recognition from those in power. Today as you face the Rome outside your front door (a community representing all strata of people), ask the Lord to give you a heart for all, opening an opportunity to share Jesus with those in your path with joyful eagerness.

Father, I want to learn from Paul's excitement—to be eager to share your Good News with anyone in my path. Thank you that the gospel is for all people. Forgive me for being afraid of sharing or being intimidated by those in power or fearful of those in a different socioeconomic position than I am. Help me be wildly enthusiastic about your ability to transform a life, starting with my own. Amen.

Day 5

Read Romans 1:16-17

I am not ashamed of this Good News about Christ. It is the power of God at work, saving everyone who believes— the Jew first and also the Gentile.

ROMANS 1:16

In a world where there are spiritual people touting hundreds of ways to know "God," while saying all ways have equal merit, sharing the gospel will bring strife. To say there is only one way to the Father who created everything is to denounce all other man-made ways, thus putting a target on yourself for ridicule. You'll be called old-fashioned, bigoted, narrow-minded, and haughty. To share the gospel is a risk.

But Paul reminds the Roman believers that this risk is also our rallying cry. The Greek word for feeling ashamed is *epaischunomai*, which connotes "being afraid, feeling shame which prevents one from doing something, a reluctance to say or do something because of fear of humiliation, experiencing a lack of courage to stand up for something."[3] We have to ask ourselves if we really, truly believe that Jesus changes everything—that the whole of history hinges on his life, death, and resurrection.

Some may be timid because they haven't yet fully explored what it means to follow Jesus. Others may fear rejection if they stand up and say they are Christ's. But if we have experienced this radical death-to-life transformation, we will find we don't care a lick about our shame.

We can't help but tell the story of our deliverance, while longing to see others experience it too. That powerful story—the story of a perfect God-man paying the penalty for our sins, then rising again—eclipses our fear. We'll see throughout the book of Romans this death-to-life scenario: We were enslaved to sin and death, then, through Jesus, we died to that old way of life to walk into newness of abundant life through the Spirit of God. This new life compels us to share. We can't help but talk about what God has done.

But we do ourselves a disservice if we forget that this gospel, this Good News, is only for those "out there." It is also for us. And we must preach it to ourselves as we walk along our daily growth journey. We must remind ourselves of our depravity without Christ as well as our daily, hourly, minute-by-minute need for his Spirit in every area of our lives, particularly our relationships. When we preach the gospel to ourselves, spiritual pride melts, a heart for others grows, we see our need for forgiveness and our obligation to pardon those who have hurt us, and that fear we have about our reputation in this world dissipates. The risk of sharing the gospel then morphs into the joyful privilege it's intended to be.

> *Father, help me let go of my fear of telling your story to others. Forgive me for the times I've been ashamed of your gospel. I know it's divisive. I know it can bring pain and strife if I share it openly. But I long for my love for you to overcome fear. In a world where absolutes are absolutely shunned, help me stand for you. And as I do, may I never stop preaching the gospel to myself. Amen.*

Day 6

Read Romans 1:18-20

*Ever since the world was created, people have seen the earth
and sky. Through everything God made, they can clearly see his
invisible qualities—his eternal power and divine nature.
So they have no excuse for not knowing God.*

Romans 1:20

As a victim of sexual abuse at the age of five, I hoped for justice. And during those agonizing moments, when I disassociated and flew up to the evergreen boughs as my rapists took turns with me, in a way I was praying to God for rescue.

Ten years later, as I sat with my back against a different evergreen tree, I first whispered my allegiance to an unseen God under a canopy of stars. I felt small under the firmament, but also beautifully loved. I'd just heard the gospel in its entirety for the first time—how Jesus had lived a sinless life, took the sins of the world upon his beautiful shoulders (and heart and body), died in my place (and yours), and then conquered the grave. And toward those faraway stars, I prayed, "God, would you be the Father that would never leave me?" As a thrice-fatherless girl, this prayer had teeth.

But prior to that night I'd had inklings, though my experience in hearing about God was limited to swear words. Instinctively, I'd known there must be a heaven and a hell. The mountains must've been shaped by something, and the sky's vastness hollered the existence of a creator.

Perhaps you have a story like mine—feeling as if you've known the story of God all along through the power of creation unfolding before you. Or maybe you experienced violation, and you wondered if that violation would ever be acknowledged or dealt with. Would justice ever come?

Romans 1:18 demonstrates the justice of God in our sin-entrenched world, while the following verses share his creative power. This idea that God is evident in both justice and creation is echoed throughout the Bible—obviously starting in Genesis. But look at how today's verses mesh hand in glove with this passage from Jeremiah:

> The LORD is the only true God. He is the living God and the everlasting King! The whole earth trembles at his anger. The nations cannot stand up to his wrath... The Lord made the earth by his power, and he preserves it by his wisdom. With his own understanding he stretched out the heavens (10:10,12).

So rest in these twin truths: God is just, and he made everything you see. That is the kind of God you can place your faith in. Why? Because he is both fair and powerful.

Father, thank you for showing everyone who you are through your justice and the way you created this world I can both see and touch. When I get discouraged about the sin all around me, the sin in me, and the sin that's harmed me, help me remember that ultimately justice will prevail. Today when I walk outside, help me find you in the nature you created, and may that bring comfort. Amen.

Day 1

Read Romans 1:21-23

They knew God, but they wouldn't worship him as God or even give him thanks. And they began to think up foolish ideas of what God was like. As a result, their minds became dark and confused.

ROMANS 1:21

You'd think that the word for *knew* in Romans 1:21 would suggest a casual acquaintance of God's or a person distant from him, but the Greek word here is *ginosko*, which means "to know by personal experience."[4] So these verses are for those who have had a personal experience with God through creation, but instead of thanking him for all he's done, "they" have turned their backs on him. Their worship, which should've been rightly directed at their Creator, is instead redirected to themselves and their own ideas—the very definition of humanism.

When humankind turns away from their Creator, the result is foolishness, lacking daily wisdom. Have you ever encountered someone who moved from bad to worse, never seeming to hit rock bottom? Just when you thought they'd touched the lowest low, they discovered a trapdoor to a lower low, and they continued to grovel, making continually bad decisions. Until we get to the bottom of ourselves, we will continually be living in this kind of darkened foolishness.

The Bible reminds us in Jeremiah 17:9 that "the human heart is the most deceitful of all things, and desperately wicked. Who really knows how bad it is?" And when we trust in our own understanding, we will be unmoored, foolish, and aimless.

What surprises most about these cautionary verses in Romans is the word *worship*. The Greek word here is *doxazo*, which simply means giving glory, in this case to God. But when we deliberately choose to worship something other than God (our choices, other people, our reputation, money, our own glory, comfort, control, and anything we want to fill our lives with besides God), we relegate him to the last place. By worshipping something other than God, we abandon the very One who created us.

These verses remind us that all of us worship something. The entirety of the world's population is spiritual, but that doesn't mean they worship God. Only those whose hearts are fully devoted to God are those who worship him. Today we have a clear choice before us: Will we pine after the things God created, or will we chase after the One who made it all?

God's heart for you is relationship. Just as a child who only approaches his parents when he wants money indicates a fractured relationship (no parent wants to be loved solely for their money), it's the same between us and God. Our worship must extend beyond simply asking him for what we want and move toward worshipping him in relationship—as the One who deserves all our affection and praise.

Father, I pray for those in my life who have turned away from worshipping you toward worshipping themselves, possessions, status, and other spiritual routes. Help them truly find rock bottom so they'll begin to build their lives on the rock that is you. Forgive me for the times I only come to you with requests instead of pausing and redirecting all my admiration your way. You are amazing, and I love you! Amen.

Day 8

Read Romans 1:24-27

*God abandoned them to do whatever shameful things their
hearts desired. As a result, they did vile and degrading things
with each other's bodies. They traded the truth about God for a
lie. So they worshiped and served the things God created instead
of the Creator himself, who is worthy of eternal praise! Amen.*

Romans 1:24-25

This world is sexually broken. And the enemy of our souls, Satan,
wants nothing more than to capitalize on this brokenness. One
of his greatest weapons against the human soul is sexual exploitation,
which epitomizes doing "vile and degrading things with each other's
bodies" (Romans 1:24). In our culture, freedom means everything is
permissible. Mainstream novels tout the so-called "beauty" of sexual
deviance. The beautiful gift God gave humanity, sexuality, has become
so tarnished and broken that we have a hard time seeing it as such.

Lust is the word that defines our culture (as well as the first-century
audience Paul addresses). And when we indulge in it, the passage says
God abandons us. To abandon, in this sense, is to hand someone over
to another powerful authority, to be transferred from being under
God's watchful care into the enslaving snare of Satan. It can also mean
handing someone over to the authorities so they can fulfill their prison
sentence. This is the opposite of the kind of "freedom" the sexually
promiscuous promise us. When deviant sexual lust overtakes our lives,
imprisonment and judgment ensue.

All this begins with a lie, and we can trace it back to the Garden of Eden, where Satan assures Eve she "will be like God" (Genesis 3:5) if she disobeys God. Except that the moment she and Adam sinned, shame horribly pierced the atmosphere, and they knew something in addition to goodness: They now knew evil, and their ability to say no to sin evaporated—they became enslaved to their new sin nature.

The problem with sexual sin is the same problem with any sin that involves idolatry (worshipping the created rather than the Creator): There is no end to its evil. Satisfaction lasts for a moment, but then you need more. Like an addict longing for the next high, as sexual deviance takes hold, you require more and more lasciviousness to gain the dopamine high. This is why porn addiction is so dangerous. It starts on the screen, but seldom ends there.

As we venture through Romans, we will see this dichotomy of worship. When we wholeheartedly worship our Creator, we experience freedom. When we replace him with anyone or anything else—such as worshipping sexual highs—slavery ensues. Paul's words are strong here particularly because he wants the Roman believers to understand and experience emancipation. So he exposes the lie that sexual "freedom" equals genuine freedom. Instead, it locks us up.

Father, I want to be free. I don't want to be enslaved to lust, no matter what form it takes. Forgive me for worshipping anything that is not you. I pray I would have purity of heart today when it comes to my sexual integrity. And I pray for those in my life who struggle in this area. Would you show them how enslaved they are? Would you woo them toward genuine freedom? Amen.

Day 9

Read Romans 1:28-32

Since they thought it foolish to acknowledge God,
he abandoned them to their foolish thinking and
let them do things that should never be done.

ROMANS 1:28

Here again we see the word *abandon*. If you have actually experienced abandonment by a loved one, you know just how harsh and painful this word can be. God loves us so much that he resorts to desperate measures to bring us back to him.

Reread this passage with the prodigal son in mind (from Luke 15:11-32). When this wayward child demands his wealth early (basically saying he wants his father dead now), and the father allows him to go, his father is abandoning him to the world. This doesn't mean the father has forsaken the child. On the contrary, he waits on the hillside, longing for his wayward child's return. In the parable, you can almost hear the echoes of the father's prayers wafting through the atmosphere into the halls of raucous living.

Because what happens to the son? He goes on to do many of the acts highlighted in this passage. He chases down sin routes, getting further and further away from his father, all the while reveling in it, celebrating it, leaning into it. And for a long season, this proud, insolent, disobedient son lives it up. He experiences the full-throttle happiness that comes from living life apart from his father.

Until the pigs. Until the slop. Until the starvation. Until the sum of his life ends in a sty. And that is the end of his sin-entrenched pilgrimage. And the father who gave his son over has one thing in mind: to eventually see restoration. If the father had accompanied the son to his debauchery, he could've rescued him, given him a soft landing, prevented pain. But it is the pain, isolated from others, that brings this boy to his senses. And when he comes home, head hung low, the father quickens his pace, restores his son, and throws a party.

God gives humankind over so they will experience the weight of their sin apart from him. So they'll see the slop, discern the hunger, realize their need. We must know our need for rescue. And, paradoxically, some can only find that when the Father lets them go for a season. Throughout the book of Romans we will see this dynamic—the absolute necessity for us to discern our lives apart from God so we will turn back to him. We have all sinned. We have all fallen short. We all need rescue. We all need a Savior.

> *Father, thank you for reminding me that I am desperately in need of you. When left to myself, I tend to run the other way, toward things I think will fill me. Before I met you, I would rather indulge my selfishness, look out for number one, than bend the knee to you. But now, today, I choose again to bow before you in gratitude for all the rescuing you've brought about since I turned toward you. You have remade my life. You have pardoned me. You have saved me. Thank you that I no longer exemplify this list of sins. Continue to change me to be more like your Son, Jesus. Amen.*

ROMANS 2

Those four words: "God gave them over"
(Romans 1:24,26,28 NASB).
I shudder under the weight.
And yet, God's kindhearted
friendship rules the day—
for which I'm utterly grateful.

BEFRIENDED

Lord, my heart isn't right
I've lost holy sight
Sin has companioned me again
But I want to be freed
Of my mountain of need
I need to befriend you again

CHORUS

It's your kindness I seek
Your faithfulness through pain
That woos my heart to be right
Spirit, transform all my fears
Would you befriend me with grace?
Oh, I need my whole life to bleed peace

Lord, I've worn a fake mask
That I'm up to the task
To live this good life in my strength
But this charade, it is ending
I want no more pretending
I long for your friendship again

BRIDGE

You're not what I thought
Love, not hatred, you brought
As I wallowed in my painful sin
You're more than my fears
So I sing through my tears
I am stunned that you call me your friend

Day 10

Read Romans 2:1-4

Since you judge others for doing these things, why do you think you can avoid God's judgment when you do the same things? Don't you see how wonderfully kind, tolerant, and patient God is with you? Does this mean nothing to you? Can't you see that his kindness is intended to turn you from your sin?

ROMANS 2:3-4

Throughout the book of Romans, we'll see pockets of kindness in reference to God, and that trait is something Jesus modeled and wants us to practice as well. Though Paul's words at the beginning of Romans 2 are stern in calling out hypocrisy, he purposefully contrasts that language with the kindness, tolerance, and patience of God.

Paul's words echo Jesus's when he warned the disciples, "You will be treated as you treat others. The standard you use in judging is the standard by which you will be judged" (Matthew 7:2). In other words, the way we judge others is the way we'll experience judgment. If we are harsh and unrelenting in our criticism, particularly if we practice the very thing we preach against, we can be assured that our sin will find us out, and that same vehemence we used to level against another will be leveled against us.

What are we to do then? Are we never to judge? Never to confront sin? According to Matthew 18:15, we are to bring up relational wrong-doing humbly: "If another believer sins against you, go privately and point out the offense. If the other person listens and confesses it, you have won that person back." So, yes, we are to talk about sin, but what Paul refers to in Romans isn't personal confrontation of relationship sin in a one-on-one conversation. He is talking about a haughty, judgmental attitude in general toward others. This kind of prideful attitude typified the Pharisees—a group of religious leaders in Jesus's day who often misunderstood the gospel and certainly missed knowing Jesus. They preferred their narrow restrictions and regulations to having a relationship with him. They preferred a harsh deity to a relationally kind one.

This advice is practical and winsome: Ask yourself how you met Jesus. How were you wooed to him? Was it through condemnation, or because of the irresistibility of Jesus? Today's passage reminds us that it's his kindness that leads us to truly repent, not his condemnation. So as you navigate your day, tuck this truth into your heart. You win more to Christ through honey than vinegar, and if you indulge in judgmental criticism, be aware that someday that same unrelenting judgment may be measured back to you.

> *Father, thank you for wooing me to yourself through kindness. I want to follow that example today, not indulging in judgment or harsh accusation, because I realize that doesn't help anyone know you. Instead, let me be unfailingly kind with those who don't yet know you. I want to be a conduit of your encouragement today, a vessel of your kindness, tolerance, and patience. You have displayed all three character traits over the course of my life, and I would love to be all three to others today. Amen.*

Day 11

Read Romans 2:5-11

There will be trouble and calamity for everyone who keeps on doing what is evil—for the Jew first and also for the Gentile. But there will be glory and honor and peace from God for all who do good—for the Jew first and also for the Gentile. For God does not show favoritism.

ROMANS 2:9-11

Why does God allow pain in this world? It's a question most Christ followers hear as someone searches to understand the problem of evil. Although today's passage seems harsh, it offers a window into the judicial nature of God, the One who will make everything right, who sees every single story, every injustice, every act of evil on this earth. Be assured, God will make things right, and that culmination of judgment will be swift and perfect.

In light of that, we must not take God lightly. Our relationship with the God who created everything cannot be superficial or fickle. It is certainly not as shallow as a junior-high crush. We touch holiness when we encounter God, the one whom Isaiah encountered, declaring, "It's all over! I am doomed, for I am a sinful man. I have filthy lips, and I live among a people with filthy lips. Yet I have seen the King, the LORD of Heaven's Armies" (6:5).

This is not a popular teaching. We would much rather see Jesus as our buddy. But if he is the One who set us right by his perfect life, sacrificial death, and powerful resurrection, then he is to be worshipped in reverence. The problem of pain becomes clearer in light of the cross. God took seriously the sin we freely indulged in against one another. Like Abraham who walked with Isaac toward a sacrifice, the Father led Jesus toward the cross. But unlike Abraham, the Father actually sacrificed his beloved Son to deal with the problem of sin.

Everyone, then, has a choice. We can bow our hearts and lives before the One who triumphed over sin and be a part of bringing light to this darkened world through the power of the Holy Spirit within us, or we can turn our backs on the One who paid it all. In the end, God will judge everyone in light of how they respond to Jesus. This is reality. This will happen. It may not be popular, but, in the end, it will be fair. Because in the final judgment, God does take seriously humankind's inhumanity toward one another. And, gratefully, he doesn't play favorites. Any one longing to know God can find him on the narrow way, no matter their situation, station, or status.

Father, I admit it's hard for me to read language about how you will judge the world someday. I'd rather skip that and think about your love. But I'm so grateful you took sin and pain seriously, that you sent your Son to die on my behalf so I could live forever. Help me be part of renewing this darkened world. Help me play a part in bringing restoration to the broken. I choose today to worship you in reverence, to take your holiness seriously. I love you. I need you. I'm humbled and grateful for all you've done. Amen.

Day 12

Read Romans 2:12-16

This is the message I proclaim—that the day is coming when God, through Christ Jesus, will judge everyone's secret life.

ROMANS 2:16

There is much written in the Gospels about the God of secrets, both positively and negatively. When we do generous acts in secret, he sees and rewards us (see Matthew 6:4). But we see the negative side of secret acts when Jesus warns, "Don't be afraid of those who threaten you. For the time is coming when everything that is covered will be revealed, and all that is secret will be made known to all" (Matthew 10:26). This second scripture is echoed in Romans 2:16. In short, what people conceal cannot be concealed forever. God sees. He knows. And he will bring all things to light.

We'll see later in Romans that 100 percent of us are guilty of sin—those who appear righteous (who hide their sin well) and those who don't. All of us need a Savior. All of us have secrets we're ashamed of, that we can't personally atone for, that we can't make right. The power of the gospel is this: All are welcome. Whether we're Jew or Gentile, whether we have the law or do not, whether we grew up in a Christian home or didn't, whether we ran far away from the Lord or stayed cautiously near, the invitation is unbiased and welcoming. We all need a Savior—someone who knows the worst parts of ourselves yet still loves us enough to die for us. This is why the gospel is good news. It is good news for those who hide (and desperately need the emancipation that comes from being real and telling the truth). And it is good news for those whose struggles are external and known. God sees both. He loves both. And he wants relationship with both.

The heart of this passage is relationship. God's heart for us is to reach out to him, to spend time with him, to obey him. He wants our hearts to be near. He wants to eradicate the secrets, renew our vision, and heal our brokenness. His love is wide and strong. It woos us toward him in reconciliation. Today you have that powerful invitation, fueled by the heartbeat of God, to come near. Will you?

> *Father, sometimes I'm scared knowing you know everything about me, even the parts of me I've concealed from others, fearing that if they found out, they'd run away. But you haven't fled. Instead, you've beckoned. Thank you. I choose right now to pursue you, to confess any hidden sin, and to experience your forgiveness and closeness. I love you. Amen.*

Day 13

Read Romans 2:17-20

You who call yourselves Jews are relying on God's law,
and you boast about your special relationship with him.

ROMANS 2:17

There's a vast gap between saying we know of someone or understand facts about a person and actually knowing him or her, right? Here we see Paul speak to his fellow Jews about their so-called relationship with God. Some were feeling proud because they'd been entrusted with the oracles of God. At Mount Sinai, after they'd been powerfully delivered from Egypt through the God-created dry bed of the Red Sea, the Jewish people received the Ten Commandments. During their disobedience, then wandering, more laws were added. Throughout the Old Testament we see a constant cycle of rebellion and returning, fickleness and faith.

The cycle we see in Judges illustrates this truth. The nation starts off well, vows to follow the law, has a leader whose heart is bent toward God, then everything devolves into chaos. They create idols, worship detestable images, and chase after foreign gods. They become adulterers, far more in love with the culture and deities of the people they conquer than they are committed to the Lord God Almighty. Then something would happen, they'd repent, return, and then they'd show fidelity again.

But this cycle never ended in outright faithfulness. Why? Many reasons. But one is this: They relied on their status as the chosen people of God and wrongly believed that following laws would mean their hearts would be right before God. We will learn throughout the book of Romans that laws can never save us. Their goal is to shine a light on our desperate need for God's salvation. In short, Israel relied on themselves, and that self-reliance led to negative cycles of disobedience, exile to Babylon, and, often, apostasy.

We are no different. If we believe that following a set of rules makes us right with God, we will fail. Our own strength will wane. Left to ourselves or our proud assertion that we are God's, we cannot live in such a way that pleases God. No matter how good we are, no matter how many "laws" we follow, we will never measure up to God's holy standard. All of this is meant to frustrate us to the point that we reach for the Lord, realizing our need for his deliverance. Galatians 3:24 reminds us, "The Law has become our tutor to lead us to Christ, so that we may be justified by faith" (NASB). The law isn't what we boast in. It cannot be what we place our faith in. It's simply the tutor that has pointed us toward our need for Christ.

Father, I don't want to glory in my own strength. I don't want to boast about my position for others to see. I realize that I cannot adhere to your law on my own. Thank you for showing me my need for a Savior. Thank you for sending Jesus as the perfect sacrifice—the sinless God-man who took on the penalty for my sins, then rose gloriously. I'm utterly grateful. Amen.

Day 14

Read Romans 2:21-24

You are so proud of knowing the law,
but you dishonor God by breaking it.
No wonder the Scriptures say,
"The Gentiles blaspheme the name
of God because of you."

ROMANS 2:23-24

How we live in this world matters because people are watching us. We often hear things like, "I'd go to church, but a bunch of hypocrites attend there." Or people hear story upon story of Christians behaving badly, and those stories then serve as reasons for them to stay away from Jesus. While we cannot control the hypocrisy of others, we can look in the mirror and see whether we're acting in a hypocritical manner.

Here Paul is speaking to Jewish believers who are saying one thing, then doing the opposite. This is a common pattern for many who are vocally vehement about sin. Isn't it ironic that those who rail against sexual sin are sometimes the ones caught in it? This is why authenticity is valued today—because so many people have been burned by heroes of the faith who said one thing (strongly) and then violated the very thing they preached against. This should not be.

The result of all this hypocritical living is that the church is maligned—but more than that, it is blasphemed. The Greek word in Romans 2:24 is obvious: *blasphemeo*. It means "to speak to harm and in general therefore means to bring into ill repute and so to slander, to defame (to harm the reputation of by libel or slander), speak evil of, to rail at (revile or scold in harsh, insolent, or abusive language and rail stresses an unrestrained berating)."[5] When we say one thing and then do the opposite, we open the door for the church to be malignantly slandered.

While we cannot change other people, we can speak up. We can grieve when a leader falls. We can share cautionary tales. We can pray for our leaders and fellow Christians, that they would not give in to temptation. We can volunteer to be a part of the restoration process (if the other person welcomes that). And, of course, we can watch our own hearts and be cautious of our boasting. We are all clay-footed folks in need of a Savior. Thankfully we have the privilege, because of what Jesus did on the cross, of repentance. Right now, in this moment, you have the opportunity to turn away from sin. Pray like this…

> *Father, I have sinned. I have railed against others commit-*
> *ting this sin while I was secretly practicing it myself. Send*
> *me a friend today to whom I can confess this sin. I don't*
> *want to be a hypocrite. I don't want to be the reason other*
> *people run away from the church. I turn away from this sin.*
> *I repent. I ask for forgiveness. And if there is someone I've*
> *wronged, give me the courage to ask them for forgiveness as*
> *well. Amen.*

Day 15

Read Romans 2:25-29

You are not a true Jew just because you were
born of Jewish parents or because you have
gone through the ceremony of circumcision.
No, a true Jew is one whose heart is right with God.

ROMANS 2:28-29

The nation of Israel was a covenant-based community. God chose them to be his own special possession. And in light of that, they were to be the city on the hill, the light shining for all to see. Their mission was to point the entire world to a relational God. Unfortunately, they didn't always fulfill this mandate. They often strayed. During Old Testament times, the Holy Spirit didn't inhabit those who believed. The Jewish people were often left to themselves to obey. And in that state, they generally obliged their innate sinful nature and fled from God.

Were many of them circumcised (a sign of the covenant)? Yes. Were they born into Judaism? Yes. Did they appear to keep the law? Yes. Were they right with God? Oftentimes, no.

In today's passage, Paul reminds the Jewish people that the outward signs of being a Jew don't truly matter. It's the inward experience of God through connected relationship that counts. God's design all along was to have a people for himself who followed him closely. This refers back to the Garden of Eden, where God, who is fully relational in the three persons of himself (the Trinity), made a decision to create image bearers of himself. We see the perfection of this in Genesis as he walked in the Garden of Eden in the cool of the evening (see 3:8). He created all of us for communion with him, to spend time with him, to be with him.

But after the fall and prior to Christ, sin marred that relationship. And no matter what humanity did, they couldn't continually walk with God. Their hearts were fickle, sin-entrenched, and broken. Though they were to shine a spotlight on God, they often found themselves rushing toward darkness. The problem came when they said they were right with God (Circumcised! In the right family! Law abiding!), but their hearts were desperately far away.

It's easy to wag our fingers at the Israelites, but we do the same thing. We go through the motions of spirituality, manage our lives without God's intervention, and live as if we are the answers to our own prayers. We may have a semblance of religiosity, but our hearts are far from him. Outward appearance does not equal a heart after God.

Thankfully we live in a time where we have constant access (like in the Garden of Eden) to our Father through the Holy Spirit who lives in us. This happened because of Jesus's perfect life, sacrificial death, and powerful resurrection on our behalf. He makes us right. He provides his presence. And he creates a pathway back to the heart of God.

Father, thank you for sending your Son to die for my sins, which are many. Show me when I'm putting on a spiritual show, pointing to my religious practices when my heart is far from you. I want to wholeheartedly pursue you, to walk with you in the cool of the evening, to hear your voice, to know you. It's not the stuff I do or the church I attend that shows I'm a follower. It's your Spirit living within me. Thank you for that great, great gift. Amen.

ROMANS 3

Our unbelief doesn't change the unchanging faithfulness of God.
It's a truth we can set our tent on—it is bedrock and strong.
I cannot help but testify to this powerful truth.

TESTIFY

We're grateful
That our struggle
Can't dethrone your faithfulness
That our lies
Cannot topple the truth

CHORUS

We all fall down
Before Christ crucified
For his renown
We throw our crown
And we testify
Yes we testify
To your scandalous, marvelous love

We're humbled
That our waywardness
Cannot obscure your ways
That our compromise
Can't nullify your promise

We're thankful
That our brokenness
Won't cause you to turn away
That our weakness
Welcomes your unending strength

BRIDGE

The just for the unjust
The King for his subjects
The right for the wrong
Oh your scandalous, marvelous love
The faithful for the faithless
The lawful for the lawless
The way for the wayward
Oh, your scandalous, marvelous love

Day 16

Read Romans 3:1-4

Some of them were unfaithful;
but just because they were unfaithful,
does that mean God will be unfaithful?
Of course not! Even if everyone
else is a liar, God is true.

ROMANS 3:3-4

Here we see Paul's argument that people's unfaithfulness doesn't mean God is equally unfaithful. In fact, the opposite is true. He cannot help but be faithful to us, even when we stray.

The nation of Israel may have deviated from the oracles of God, although they experienced his presence, provision, protection, and direction. Even though they knew God's laws, they continued to be fickle, pursuing other gods. This is entirely a reflection upon the sinfulness we all have in our Adam-and-Eve-given sin DNA, but it does not convict God of faithlessness. In fact, in 2 Timothy 2:13, we see this underscored: "If we are unfaithful, he remains faithful, for he cannot deny who he is."

As I read Romans every day for ninety days, one of the things I did was mark up the text, using different colored pens for different types of language. For anything to do with court, law, lawyers, and justice, I used green. Romans bleeds green, and verse 4 starts the trend with a quote from Psalm 51:4, which says, "Against you, and you alone, have I sinned; I have done what is evil in your sight. You will be proved right in what you say, and your judgment against me is just." These are King David's words to God after Nathan the prophet confronted him about his sins against Bathsheba and Uriah. David recognizes his offense and owns up to it, the very nature of the repentance necessary to approach God after sin. He models to the nation of Israel what it looks like, though so few followed his man-after-God's-heart example. He concludes by basically saying, "I did wrong, but God is right."

In the first few verses of Romans 3, the apostle Paul is beginning his grand argument regarding all believers—that we share the sin DNA of all humanity, and we're in desperate need of a Savior. But there's a judicial problem. We, as broken, sinful people, cannot approach the Judge in the divine court of law. Like David, we did wrong, but God is right. Eventually Paul unfolds the grand solution to our sin problem—Jesus taking upon himself our sins to satisfy the law court. On the cross, he paid the just penalty for our sins, opening the door wide to heaven's joy and God's presence. The gospel is simply that: we did wrong, but God is right, and his Son made us right.

In other words, your unfaithfulness cannot negate God's nature, which exudes faithfulness. Jesus was faithful unto death—for our sakes and God's glory. And now our job is to rest in that and live out our lives in Holy Spirit-infused gratitude!

> *Father, thank you for your powerfully judicious act of sending your Son to the cross. I confess I have done wrong, thought wrong, believed wrong, but you are right. You are always right, and you have made me right with you. Teach me what it means to live out my life in gratitude for all you've done. I'm astounded, surprised, grateful, and amazed. Amen.*

Day 17

Read Romans 3:5-8

*"But," some might say, "our sinfulness serves a good purpose,
for it helps people see how righteous God is. Isn't it unfair,
then, for him to punish us?" (This is merely a human point
of view.) Of course not! If God were not entirely fair,
how would he be qualified to judge the world?*

ROMANS 3:5-6

God is entirely fair.

As the omniscient One, he sees every angle of every situation. He knows the bit players and the con men (and women), as well as the secret motives of all people's hearts. He is the Creator of all that we see, and he has fashioned every human being in their mothers' wombs. Because of his power and creativity, alongside his sovereign rule over the universe (he's even named every star; see Psalm 147:4), he is able to rightly discern and judge with complete fairness.

But Paul has encountered people along his church-planting journeys who have argued with him about sin and fairness and glory. Their clever argument went something like this: "If my sin (darkness) helps God's righteousness (light) shine all the more in glory, then what are we worrying about? You need darkness to better highlight the light, right?" Later in Romans 6:1-2, Paul reframes this same argument: "Should we keep on sinning so that God can show us more and more of his wonderful grace? Of course not! Since we have died to sin, how can we continue to live in it?"

Sin is not something to boast about or indulge in. More sin isn't something to revel in, but to repent of. The hyper-grace movements in recent history seem to be putting forth the same argument: Sin is no big deal because grace covers it all. This type of belief has been repudiated throughout the ages, but a particularly well-articulated rebuttal comes from Dietrich Bonhoeffer, who wrote this in *The Cost of Discipleship*: "Cheap grace is the preaching of forgiveness without requiring repentance, baptism without church discipline, Communion without confession, absolution without personal confession. Cheap grace is grace without discipleship, grace without the cross, grace without Jesus Christ, living and incarnate."[6]

Our egregious sin cost Jesus his life. Grace is costly, and because it is, our lives become spilled-out offerings to him. We stay close to the Lord through the power of the Holy Spirit, choosing to repent of sin and walk in grace.

> *Father, help me remember that sin is a big deal, that it cost the life of your Son. I don't want to trample on your grace. While I understand that your grace abounds when I repent of my sin, I don't want to live in sin anymore. Instead, let my life reflect the radical change the Spirit has inaugurated in me. I love you. I appreciate all you've done. And I sit here in awe of you—your strength, knowledge, and creative powers. Amen.*

Day 18

Read Romans 3:9-18

Should we conclude that we Jews are better than others?
No, not at all, for we have already shown that all people,
whether Jews or Gentiles, are under the power of sin.

ROMANS 3:9

Paul knows the ancient texts well, and he quotes from several psalms and the book of Isaiah in this passage (see Psalms 5:9; 10:7; 14:1-3; 36:1; 53:1-3; 140:3; and Isaiah 59:7-8). He is steeped in them, knows them like he knows his own gait. He, as a Jew, makes the case that the gospel is for all people—not simply the nation of Israel. In fact, God's plan all along has been to coax all the nations to himself. He started by creating humankind in the garden in order that they rightly relate to him.

When sin entered in, humanity experienced a fatal infection—a seemingly incurable condition that ends in physical death. Although the nation of Israel experienced God's guidance and favor, even they rebelled and fell away from God through many eras—judges, kings, prophets, and exile. It wasn't until Jesus lived perfectly, died in our place, then conquered the foe of death that God's plan culminated.

And that plan includes you, me, and everyone—not simply people with a Jewish lineage. Why? Because all humankind suffers from the fall. We are all sinners. No one does what is right in their own heart. When it comes to Jew and Gentile, we are all on equally bad footing, full of sin, separated from God, in need of redemption.

Enter Jesus. He is a Jew, but one who obeys every jot and tittle of the law. He exemplifies the opposite of these Old Testament verses. Instead of unrighteousness, his DNA is righteousness. Instead of foolish thoughts and behavior, he personifies wisdom. He did not turn away; instead, he turned toward the cross—as a useful, needed sacrifice. He's known as the Good Shepherd. His words are truth and life. No venom leaves his lips, only encouragement and apt words for every moment, every heart. While others cursed him, and bitter hearts sent him to his death, he did not retaliate in kind. He's the giver of life, yet he suffered murder at the hands of others, silently, resolutely. His kingdom is the opposite of destruction and misery—it is the epitome of creative rejuvenation and joy. He is the Prince of Peace who feared God the Father throughout his days on earth.

This Jesus reconciled us to himself, gave freely of his life, and showed us the way to live. Let's praise him for that.

Father, I'm in awe of Jesus. All he did. How he obeyed. How he didn't retaliate or heap abuse on others when he suffered. He is the example I want to follow, the heart I want to pursue. Teach me to be like him—peace-filled, alert to your ways, full of life and laughter, able to say words that change people's difficult days. Help me walk in truth today, admitting it to myself, sharing it with those who need it. Amen.

Day 19

Read Romans 3:19-20

No one can ever be made right with God by doing what the law commands. The law simply shows us how sinful we are.

ROMANS 3:20

I am a rule follower to my core. Give me a good list of rules, and my palms sweat in joyful anticipation. The problem often comes when I can no longer adhere to every rule perfectly. Which is all the time. Because who can? Still, there is a feeling of control I get when I list, then follow, rules. When life grows chaotic, and I feel like the world spins off-kilter, the way I cope is through legalism. It's safe. It's counted. It's black and white.

But it has nothing to do with relationship.

Let's say I create a list of "How to Be the Best Wife" rules to show how I love my husband. I follow them to a T, or at least I try. I make coffee for my husband, anticipate his daily needs, and by rote tell him, "I love you," seven times a day at prescribed times. But on weary days, those pre-decided sentiments feel more and more like obligation. Although my initial goal was good—I wanted to demonstrate love to my husband—the end of it all becomes lifeless. The obligation strangles spontaneity, and I begin to resent my husband, the rules I've created, and my robotic rhythm.

No one wants to love because they're forced to, nor does anyone want to be the recipient of determination-based rule following. So in light of today's text, how are we to view the law? Does it bring life? No. Does it enhance our relationship with God? No. Did it empower the nation of Israel to love God more fully? No. Then why would God send it? The answer lies in Romans 3:20. The law reveals that we cannot accomplish life without God. In our own strength, we fail. We are cursed with the sin infection, something inherited by our forefather and foremother in the Garden of Eden. This law was simply a measuring stick to reveal our need for help. It showed us our depravity apart from our Creator, and it wooed us toward Jesus.

A relationship with God is not really a relationship if it is solely based on us following all the rules—for two reasons. One, we cannot follow all the rules in our own strength anyway, so it's a no-win situation. Two, no one likes to be in a relationship tied up by regulations. It's like forcing your kids to say they're sorry to each other when they're clearly not sorry. The law, then, is what God put in place to draw us to himself. It reveals our sin and our utter helplessness to conquer it. And it produces in us a longing for his deliverance. Jesus fulfilled the law, being the perfection of humanity, then provided the once-and-for-all sacrifice needed to satisfy the justice of God. His life, death, and resurrection fulfilled the requirements of the law for all of us, and now we can pursue him in relationship out of gratitude, not rote obligation.

Father, thank you for sending your Son to die for me, for us, for the world. While it may seem easier to create laws and rules when I follow you, that kind of religion has little to do with relationship and everything to do with my need for control. I acknowledge that apart from Christ's work on the cross, I am lost. I need you. Every day. And I want to love you in relationship, as a celebration of all you've done for me. Amen.

Day 20

Read Romans 3:21-26

*We are made right with God by placing our faith
in Jesus Christ. And this is true for everyone
who believes, no matter who we are.*

ROMANS 3:22

Throughout the book of Romans, we see Paul using the word *faith* generously. The word here is *pistis*, which means "a strong and welcome conviction or belief that Jesus is the Messiah, through whom we obtain eternal salvation in the kingdom of God."[7] As Paul asserts, we are made right with God because of what Jesus did.

This is a stated fact of justice, enacted in the heavenly law court. We, the defendants, are guilty of the many sins we commit over our lifetimes. The fact of our guilt cannot be refuted. We are guilty. We have no defense, certainly no excuse. But Christ became both our defense attorney and the means by which we are set free. He approached the righteous Judge (God the Father), saying, "I will pay the penalty for all the sins they committed." And then he did just that, bleeding forgiveness from the common-day Roman "justice" device—the cross. He paid for our sins in full—something we could never do. And now we are set free to live our lives in gratitude.

We are made right (also known as "being righteous") because of Jesus's righteous act. This is a stated, completed act we can rest in and place our faith in. Our thankfulness to God, then, is our *pistis*, our belief that his death happened, it satisfied the requirements of the law (the shedding of blood), and it inaugurated a brand-new way of living—not in the frustration of trying in vain to follow the law, but in the newness of responding to the Holy Spirit who now resides within us. From guilty to pardoned. From enslaved to set free. From darkness to light. Having faith simply means believing these outrageously beautiful truths.

> *Father, how can I thank you for all you've done? You sent your Son to die in my place. You secured my position as your child in the heavenly law court. I am set free. I am made new. I am well loved by you. Thank you. Help me live in light of all these powerful truths today. Help me no longer rehash my sins and live in condemnation, but instead live a life of faith and thankfulness. Amen.*

Day 21

Read Romans 3:27-31

*Can we boast, then, that we have done anything to be accepted
by God? No, because our acquittal is not based on obeying
the law. It is based on faith. So we are made right with
God through faith and not by obeying the law.*

Romans 3:27-28

Notice the continued legal language Paul uses here. We are acquitted. We are made right. On what basis? Faith—a strong-held belief in Jesus's sacrifice on the cross. And Paul adds something important in verse 31: "Only when we have faith do we truly fulfill the law." So faith is the actual language of acquittal.

What is beautiful about this statement is whom it's offered to. The nation of Israel wrongly misinterpreted their calling. They were to be a beacon, representing God to the world. Why? To woo others to himself. But they neglected their mission. They became muddied (much like the rest of us do) by the surrounding culture's idols. Yet they also thrived in an us-versus-them community, viewing everyone else as outsiders. Their insider culture mitigated their mandate, and they became proud of their stature with God, yet rebellious in their day-to-day actions. They, too, needed a Savior.

But this being made right is not only offered to the nation of Israel. It is also offered freely to the entire world. The famous verse, John 3:16, echoes this truth, as do the following verses.

This is how God loved the world: He gave his one and only Son, so that everyone who believes in him will not perish but have eternal life. God sent his Son into the world not to judge the world, but to save the world through him. There is no judgment against anyone who believes in him. But anyone who does not believe in him has already been judged for not believing in God's one and only Son. And the judgment is based on this fact: God's light came into the world, but people loved the darkness more than the light, for their actions were evil (3:16-19).

Note how often *believing* (a synonym for "having faith") is mentioned here—four times. And also see whom God comes to redeem—all of mankind, not simply the Jewish people. This gift is for all; it is openly given. Our job, then, is simply to believe.

We tend to make things complicated. We tack all sorts of requirements to Christianity like a strange game of pin the tail on the donkey. But the simplicity and purity of the gospel is this: Christ died for the entire world, and we must believe that.

Father, thank you for loving the entire world. Thank you for having a plan from the beginning to bring the whole world to yourself. Thank you for sending Jesus to die on behalf of all sinners. Thank you that the requirement you have for me is simply faith—to trust in what you've done. Help me not to complicate it. Help me live out the mandate you had for the nation of Israel—to be a light that highlights you to a world in need of your salvation. Amen.

ROMANS 4

In the storms of life, we can still believe.

I WANT TO BELIEVE

When the wind and the sea
Hurl rocks at my days
I cower and pray
"Lord, please take this strife"
Yet the storms rage their fast-moving plans

CHORUS
I want to believe
In the midst of the storms
I want to believe
In the night, in the morn
I want to believe

When I can't see the way
I want to believe
I can't seem to believe
My way hazily through
I need all of your strength
To be made beautifully new
Yet the night
Chases away my resolve

When blustery tempests
Threaten all of my steps
On tenacious hope, I will stand
Lord, keep my feet on a steadier pace
While the wind and the seas salt my tears

BRIDGE
My faith isn't strong
But you blessedly are
My hope isn't fixed
But your promises are
My joy, incomplete
Yet you completed my heart
My belief, oh it wavers
But your love, unwavering
You are everything I'm not
I believe. I believe.

Day 22

Read Romans 4:1-3

The Scriptures tell us, "Abraham believed God, and God counted him as righteous because of his faith."

ROMANS 4:3

Patriarch: That's what Abraham is called. He was the pioneer of the nation of Israel, the founder who left everything he knew to sojourn in a place he didn't yet know in order to produce a family of people who were to become the apple of God's eye—all while experiencing an extremely long bout of infertility. It all seemed absolutely impossible, this quest. But he persisted. He continued his trek. He believed what God told him.

Today's verse is a direct quotation from Genesis 15:6. To understand its context, watch the interaction between Abraham (called Abram at the time) and God:

> The LORD spoke to Abram in a vision and said to him, "Do not be afraid, Abram, for I will protect you, and your reward will be great." But Abram replied, "O Sovereign LORD, what good are all your blessings when I don't even have a son? Since you've given me no children, Eliezer of Damascus, a servant in my household, will inherit all my wealth. You have given me no descendants of my own, so one of my servants will be my heir." Then the LORD said to him, "No, your servant will not be your heir, for you

will have a son of your own who will be your heir." Then the LORD took Abram outside and said to him, "Look up into the sky and count the stars if you can. That's how many descendants you will have!" And Abram believed the LORD, and the LORD counted him as righteous because of his faith (15:1-6).

Abram (literally "father of height"), who later is named Abraham ("the father of a multitude"), initially started his conversation with reality and sight. His reality? He had no children. What he saw? Eliezer of Damascus, his servant. In light of reality and sight, there were no logical solutions. But God interrupted logic by declaring what would be (the impossible, a son), then beckoning Abram to view the stars. God lifted his gaze from reality and sight to the impossibly high heavens. And that's when Abram believed.

Perhaps you need the same. Your reality seems fixed. You see no solution forward. Listen to the voice of God echoing through Scripture. He is the God of the impossible. He is the God of possibility amid impossibility. And he asks us to lift our heads to the myriad of stars he flung with ease into existence. This is the God you can trust. This is the God you can have faith in.

> *Father, help me hear your voice in the midst of your word today. I want to believe you like Abram did. I love that you elevate faith here, that you value my trust in you more than you value my ability to follow you. Help me build my trust muscle. I choose to lift my gaze to the heavens today, to be reminded of your vast capabilities. I am incapable of fixing my situation, but you are capable. I trust you. Amen.*

Day 23

Read Romans 4:4-8

When people work, their wages are not a gift, but something
they have earned. But people are counted as righteous,
not because of their work, but because of their faith
in God who forgives sinners.

ROMANS 4:4-5

Again we see this theme of faith expounded on by Paul. Faith is important. God values it. Yet so many times we fail in this area of belief and trust. We think, wrongly, that we must work to secure our future. We must strive to make everything right. We must connive to win approval. We must perform to become perfect.

Yet we are sinners—down to our core. And no amount of work can change that identity. The only way to transfer our identity from sinner to saint (and yes, that is who we are once we follow Jesus) is having "faith in God who forgives sinners" (Romans 4:5).

This emphasis on faith pushes against a karmic society that wrongly believes we get what's coming to us, or, conversely, we'll reap rewards if we're nice. Various aberrational thoughts that masquerade as "Christian" support this lie. We see it in the health and wealth gospel—that if we say the right mantra of prayers, God is obligated, like a jukebox in the sky, to play the song we paid (prayed) for. Or if we speak positive words to the universe, it will be obligated to repay us in goodness. This, of course, relates to the reality of an unearned salvation, but doesn't mean we should throw caution out the window and sin like crazy in light of our great redemption. Scripture is clear (see Galatians 6:7-10 or read the Book of Proverbs) that we will reap what we sow. Because of our gratitude toward the God who rescued us, we naturally long to please him. The motivation for our obedience is love, not conniving to impress God into giving us reward. The reward—salvation—is already gloriously settled.

We must be wise and discerning. There is no way to make good things happen to us by our good works. We can certainly try. Some people have made it their life's ambition. They'll say things like, "I'll make it into heaven because I'm a good person," misunderstanding the power of their sinful nature.

Here we are reminded that working for good may earn a paycheck, but it will not earn salvation. No one can do such a thing. No mud hill of good works atones for the mountain peak of sin against a holy God. The gap between the two is insurmountable. No, this is an unfair exchange, where God sent his Son to pay every last penalty for our sin. Jesus did the hard work on the cross. And we reap the positive consequences—his goodness exchanged for our salvation. King David glimpsed it on tiptoes from afar when he experienced the pardon of God. He speaks of the utter joy that comes in pardon. Instead of karma imposing a rightful penalty for David's sins, God intervened in his life, delivered him from sin, then expunged his rap sheet. All sheer gift, something David could never, ever earn.

We are the same. God has graced us. And our response should simply be utter gratitude.

Father, I am amazed. You are good. You have done a good work so I could be pardoned. Thank you for sending Jesus to pay the penalty I never could. Thank you that your kingdom is not based on karma, but on compassion. Thank you that I don't have to work-work-work to secure my security. Instead, I rest in what you've already done. I love you. Amen.

Day 24

Read Romans 4:9-12

Circumcision was a sign that Abraham already had faith and that God had already accepted him and declared him to be righteous—even before he was circumcised. So Abraham is the spiritual father of those who have faith but have not been circumcised. They are counted as righteous because of their faith.

ROMANS 4:11

Paul reminds his Gentile and Jewish audience that salvation is for all. This passage cements that truth. Here we see Abraham believing God, then later being circumcised. The circumcision was a ceremony of covenant—it commemorated the agreement between God and Abraham and the inevitable nation of Israel. God would be their God, and they would be his people. You see the promise here:

> The LORD had said to Abram, "Leave your native country, your relatives, and your father's family, and go to the land that I will show you. I will make you into a great nation. I will bless you and make you famous, and you will be a blessing to others. I will bless those who bless you and curse those who treat you with contempt. All the families on earth will be blessed through you" (Genesis 12:1-3).

This covenant pre-shouted the gospel. Through one man (Abraham) all would be blessed. This promise of coming blessing wasn't merely for those who would become the Jewish people, but it would be for every single family on earth, and that reality would come to beautiful fruition through one man, Jesus.

And we see other similarities. God spoke. Abraham believed. God confirmed the covenant. Abraham was circumcised (an action that revealed his faith in what God would do). In the New Testament, God speaks clearly through Jesus Christ. We believe after we hear about his perfect life, sacrifice, and overcoming the sting of death. God confirms this new covenant by sending us the Holy Spirit. And then we choose to be baptized based on our faith in what God has done and will do in our lives.

God speaks. We believe. He confirms. We act. And as Paul's narrative so powerfully shows us, these patterns remind us that God is the great initiator of it all. He is the center of the story, not us. He is the one who rescues. He does what we cannot. And he welcomes all people, Jewish and non-Jewish, into this life of faith.

> *Father, wow. I love that there are such clear patterns throughout your word. Thank you that your rescue is for me as well as Abraham's family. Thank you for doing all the heavy lifting in regard to my salvation. You have done so much. You have said so much. You have accomplished so much. My response is simply to obey you today. My obedience shows my joyful surrender to your ways. Amen.*

Day 25

Read Romans 4:13-17

Abraham is the father of all who believe. That is what the Scriptures mean when God told him, "I have made you the father of many nations." This happened because Abraham believed in the God who brings the dead back to life and who creates new things out of nothing.

ROMANS 4:16-17

Go through this passage and count the amount of times the word *faith* or *believe* are used. You'll find those powerful words six times. Paul's emphasis here is not on the impossibility of obeying the law perfectly; it's on the importance of faith. Of believing in the ability of God rather than our limited capability. Throughout Romans you'll see this strong emphasis. It's not about us doing good deeds to be noticed by God. It's not about writing down Christian to-do lists, then beautifully adhering to them.

In short, our Christianity is not about us. It's about the object of our faith: the Lord Jesus Christ. And he is utterly dependable, completely reliable, wholly God, powerfully empathetic, and the One who secured our eternity. We cannot rely on ourselves to accomplish such a feat. We personally cannot bridge the wide chasm between a holy God and a sin-entrenched people. Only Jesus, with his perfect atoning sacrifice, can do that.

So our job is simple: to have faith. To believe that Jesus paid everything, that we are the grateful paupers who are the recipients of his costly grace. To have faith that he can create something beautiful out of nothing. He can raise the dead. He can create life. He can inaugurate galaxies. He can run the universe while we nap.

Faith isn't about us. It's about him. And if we truly want to know what kind of life pleases him, we can simply look at Abraham the patriarch, who radically believed that God could create a nation from a closed womb, who later trusted God to resurrect his only son. These are powerful, important lessons for all of us. Faith is what matters because God's abilities to transform and renew overpower everything.

> *Father, forgive me when I think that my faith is up to me. It's actually all about you—your abilities, your power, your miracles. Instead of fretting about my insecurities and failures, help me shift my focus to you—the powerful originator and recipient of my faith. You are faithful. You are good. And I choose today to believe you, to trust you, to entrust my life to you. Amen.*

Day 26

Read Romans 4:18-25

*Even when there was no reason for hope, Abraham kept
hoping—believing that he would become the father of
many nations. For God had said to him, "That's how many
descendants you will have!" And Abraham's faith did not
weaken, even though, at about 100 years of age, he figured his
body was as good as dead—and so was Sarah's womb.
Abraham never wavered in believing God's promise.
In fact, his faith grew stronger, and in
this he brought glory to God.*

ROMANS 4:18-20

This passage has puzzled me because I remember the times Abraham did seem to doubt. He produced an heir through his wife's servant Hagar. This certainly was circumventing belief by taking matters into his own hands. There were times he put his wife, Sarah, into compromising situations out of fear of what could happen because of her desirable beauty and the fickleness of kings. But as I talked about this to my husband, Patrick, he reminded me of the progression of belief Abraham experienced, particularly in regard to Hagar. Even though he chose that route, he continued to choose the pathway of trust. And, eventually, the impossible happened.

Isn't that the way of faith? We are broken people, prone to doubt God. We take matters into our own hands out of fear. We try to navigate life on our own terms. Yet God doesn't give up on us. He still guides us, gently leading us toward himself. He continues to answer our prayers despite our doubt. And when we see his faithfulness come to fruition, in the end, our faith is radically strengthened.

There is solace in knowing that, besides Jesus, there is no human being in the Bible who perfectly walked out faith. Yet God counts our seed of faith as if it were already the plant. He sees our journey from beginning to end, while we mire ourselves in the mucky middle. What a faithful God we serve! He doesn't penalize us for missteps or doubt. He doesn't revoke his promises based on our own lack of faith. No, he presses on with his plan, despite our frailty.

And now, because of Jesus, we are counted as righteous because we believe in him. That is sheer gift, pure grace, audacious love—in action. This again proves to us that our Christianity is about Christ, not about us. All glory goes to the One who makes us right, even while we were helpless to save ourselves.

Father, thank you for the example of Abraham, who seemingly wavered, but you still used him, provided Isaac, and walked with him. I'm thankful you continue to use me, that you don't give up on me even though there are times I lack faith and need constant reassurance of your presence. I revere you today for sending Jesus to die for my sins. I give you glory. It's not about me and my faith as much as it is about you and your faithfulness. Amen.

ROMANS 5

We are all a conundrum of will and failure,
a paradox of longing to love the
Lord and running away.
This is my ode to the dichotomy.

TURNING

Turn my suffering to endurance
Turn endurance into character
Turn my character to hope
Turn my hope into glory

CHORUS

Pour out your love
Let it cascade over me
Through your Spirit alive within
I am washed wholly clean
You have perished in my place
Bore the weight of my disgrace
By your grace I will stand tall
You tore down the dividing wall

Turn my helplessness to trust
Turn that trust to forgiveness
Turn forgiveness into love
Turn all love into new faith

Turn my sorrow into joy
Turn that joy into your peace
Turn that peace to pardoning
Turn my pardon to worship

BRIDGE

I was helpless
Yet you rescued
Sin had severed
Yet you rescued
Me, your enemy
Yet you rescued
I was peaceless
Yet you rescued

Day 21

Read Romans 5:1-5

Because of our faith, Christ has brought us into this place
of undeserved privilege where we now stand, and we
confidently and joyfully look forward to sharing God's glory.
We can rejoice, too, when we run into problems and trials,
for we know that they help us develop endurance. And
endurance develops strength of character, and character
strengthens our confident hope of salvation.

ROMANS 5:2-4

What powerful words smashed together: *undeserved privilege.* They so perfectly capture what it means to be a Christ follower. We are the recipients of divine grace, the beneficiaries of a gift that cannot be earned. We have been made right, though we've been wrong and have wronged others and a holy God.

Because of all this audacious inclusion, this welcoming party God throws for us, we can have confidence and joy—even in the midst of inevitable trials and pain. The pathway toward this kind of confident living is our faith—our trust in a God who is both powerful and personal.

The truth is we will face trials. It's normative in the Christian life to experience them. Jesus warned us that we would face them. "I have told you all this so that you may have peace in me. Here on earth you will have many trials and sorrows. But take heart, because I have overcome the world" (John 16:33). Trials and troubles are universal to all human beings, but the peace of Jesus is reserved for those who truly follow him. You have a gift, friend: the powerful and personal presence of Christ. He will walk with you in your pain, while trials mount, when hope fades. He has overcome this crazy world. He has conquered death. He has made a way for you. He grants peace in the chaos.

The progression is instructive: Jesus's presence in trials produces endurance. The more we endure, the stronger our character matures. And as the Spirit develops character in us, the more we hope for what we do not see—the coming kingdom of God, where all things are made right. This is the kind of hope that cannot disappoint because it's based on future reality, and our down payment is the Spirit living and breathing within us. Though we struggle to understand his love, the Spirit helps us know the reality of it every single day.

> *Father, wow. Thank you. In the midst of my current trial, I pray that you would empower me to endure with joy. I long to have this current struggle produce strength of character. In other words, I want to endure this trial better than I did the last trial. I want to trust you more and have less anxiety and more belief. And you promise that the result of all this is hope. I could use a deeper experience of biblical hope today. Amen.*

Day 28

Read Romans 5:6-11

Since our friendship with God was restored by the death of his Son while we were still his enemies, we will certainly be saved through the life of his Son. So now we can rejoice in our wonderful new relationship with God because our Lord Jesus Christ has made us friends of God.

ROMANS 5:10-11

The word for enemies here is *echthros,* and it is used 32 times in the New Testament. One typical example is found in Matthew 5:43-44, where Jesus tells us to love our enemies and pray for those who persecute us. These are people you have enmity with, those you really don't like, and are often people who serve as adversaries to you. Here the word is used to describe all of us in our relationship with God. "*Echthros* is one who has the extreme negative attitude that is the opposite of love and friendship. An enemy is one that is antagonistic to another; especially seeking to injure, overthrow, or confound the opponent. Scripture often uses *echthros* as a noun describing 'the adversary,' Satan! Like father like son!"[8]

Knowing just how enemy-like our sin has made us to a holy God should deepen our gratitude for God, who sent his Son for the sole purpose of turning enemies into friends. When Paul asserts, "Our friendship with God was restored by the death of his Son" (Romans 5:10), he uses the word *katallasso* that simply means to make change or to be reconciled. In other words, it's a banking term, an exchange of goods.[9] Jesus exchanged his life for ours, his death for our emancipation.

It's almost too much to take in—that the God who made us stooped to become like us, exchanging his perfect life for our deeply imperfect, enemy-like life. We were not friends before this exchange. We were hostile toward God, and yet he still enacted this rescue mission where he lost everything, yet gained our reconciliation.

To be called a friend of God is no small thing. To move from hostility to friendship is radical and humbling. And that is why we read Jesus's words in Matthew about loving our enemies. He is only asking us to do what he has already done. When we love those who don't love us, when we pursue through prayer those who have wronged us, when we forgive those who have hurt us, we are acting like our Savior.

> *Father, I can scarcely take it all in, this redemption. I understand I was your enemy, your foe—because of the sin that so easily entangled me. And yet, you sent your Son to die on my behalf. I pray today that I would live in gratitude over that stunning act, and that your pardon of me would inform the way I pray for and pardon others in my life. Help me love my enemies and pray for those who persecute me today. Amen.*

Day 29

Read Romans 5:12-17

The result of God's gracious gift is very different from the result of that one man's sin. For Adam's sin led to condemnation, but God's free gift leads to our being made right with God, even though we are guilty of many sins.

ROMANS 5:16

The Greek word for the first instance of *gift* in Romans 5:16 is *dorema*, the same word James uses in James 1:17: "Whatever is good and perfect is a gift coming down to us from God our Father, who created all the lights in the heavens. He never changes or casts a shifting shadow." It is an unearned grace, a surprise present bestowed freely. But just because it is given freely does not mean it costs nothing.

Adam and Eve started the sin ball rolling, infecting everyone with the propensity to rebel against God and take life into our own hands. Instead of submitting ourselves to the authorship of God, we took the pen from him and started writing our stories without him. Sin causes all of us to live as rebels in God's grand narrative. But there's a beautiful plot twist. Though our tragedy trajectory seemed utterly helpless—that we were enslaved to sin forever—God's gift through Jesus Christ shifted everything, turning tragedy to triumph.

Yes, through mankind's rebellion, we were all subject to sin, but that makes God's great reversal all the more stunning. We've moved from guilty to not guilty, from enslaved to free, from powerless against sin to being empowered to fight it. Our story has changed from dead man walking to liberated former-prisoner. The word for "being made right"—or "justification" in other translations—is *dikaioma*, and it's "used in this verse to signify the clearing of one of a violation as an act of justification and equates with the removal of guilt or granting of an acquittal."[10] Guilt was ours, but it is no longer our story. Let's thank God for that.

> *Father, I am free! You have set me right. Forgive me for trying to write my own story, for living for myself, for indulging in sin. Once again I turn away from that and fully face Jesus, who secured my justification. I want to live a new story with you as my author and me as your grateful recipient of audacious grace. Thank you that nothing can alter my new state of being made right. It is finished, and I am free! Amen.*

Day 30

Read Romans 5:18-21

Just as sin ruled over all people and brought them to death,
now God's wonderful grace rules instead,
giving us right standing with God
and resulting in eternal life through
Jesus Christ our Lord.

ROMANS 5:21

For millennia, sin reigned. Its power over humanity remained deadlocked and strong. We were helpless to do anything about our propensity to choose ourselves over the will of God. Helpless, hapless, and hardened, humanity stumbled blindly. But when Christ intersected our cosmos, walked the earth sinlessly, and showed us what right-with-God living looks like, everything changed. His life, death, and resurrection became the earthquake that rocked that long-lived paradigm.

And now this: *charis basileuse*. Grace reigns. It rules.

Charis means unmerited grace. It is God's sheer gift to us, full of pardoning love and unearned affection.

Combined with *basileuo*, grace takes on deeper meaning. The word is derived from the Greek word for *king*. Grace is powerful. It is the weapon wielded by a king. It's more than a handout or a hand up. It is the "rule of the Messiah" that exercises "the highest influence."[11]

There is a spiritual battle raging all around us. We have a very real enemy, Satan, who lies, kills, destroys, and steals from us. He is

empowered by sin, intent on entangling us in it, and powerfully conniving. But though he cackled his joy as Jesus hung his sacred head and
died, he cowered when Jesus rose again because, in that instant, grace
ruled. The reign of King Jesus began as he gathered his spoils of war
(us!) and set us free from Satan's ill-intentioned captivity. Our good
King fought sin's war and won. And now we live in newness of life, no
longer ensnared, freed from captivity.

Let the truth of *Grace rules* permeate your life today. Grace is not
weak; it is an indication that your King, powerful and strong, has rescued you.

> *Father, thank you for sending your Son to be the conquer-
> ing King. Thank you for being a victorious God, reigning
> over sin and death. Help me live in light of grace ruling
> that way in my life. Powerfully strengthen me. Remind me
> afresh what you've rescued me from. I don't want to live
> deterred, chasing sin and succumbing to the tricks of my
> very real enemy. Instead, let grace rule and reign in my life
> today. Amen.*

ROMANS 6

It stuns me to silence every time I think of the courtroom,
Jesus as my defender and the One who took my place.

NEVER-ENDING, AUDACIOUS GRACE

It's cold in the courtroom of my sinful life
I shake while considering my mountain of guilt
That ushered me into this place desolate
Guilty, I wait

CHORUS
How can I thank you for taking my place?
How can I possibly sing enough praise?
How can I live a new life that is worthy
Of your never-ending, audacious grace?

In a hiccup of time, you choose to sit near
My sin dousing you like a cascade of shame
I feel its coldness as it shivers your heart
Shaking, I wait

You stood in my place while the Judge read the verdict
Took all of the punishment I rightly deserved
Wearing my guilt, you died as you offered
Your life, for mine

I no longer wear the garments of judgment
I'm set free by the One who has paid it in full
No longer a slave to things that destroyed me
Unshackled, I rise

Death holds no victory over such resurrection
You conquered the grave, ushering raucous, new life
Alive with you now, I let go of transgression
Awakened, I live

I do not deserve such a lavish reception
From prison to wide open spaces, I stand
You rescued my heart from sin's broken deception
Welcomed, I dance

Day 31

Read Romans 6:1-4

Should we keep on sinning so that God can show us more and more of his wonderful grace? Of course not! Since we have died to sin, how can we continue to live in it? Or have you forgotten that when we were joined with Christ Jesus in baptism, we joined him in his death?

ROMANS 6:1-3

Baptism is an outward sign of an inward, vital reality. It's a physical demonstration of what happened to us the moment we met Christ for the first time, when we asked him to be the Lord of everything in our lives. In that act of initial surrender, we essentially said that the way life had been would be no more, and we would be living a brand-new life. Our propensity to live on our own terms was replaced with a sincere desire to honor God in everything we do—not out of rote obligation to win brownie points, but out of sheer joy for what Christ already did for us.

His life, death, and resurrection are the rhythms of our life now. He lived, so we can, though the Spirit within us, emulate the love-filled life he led. He died, so we might learn to die to ourselves. He rose, so we could live with renewed hope and a joyful view of the kingdom of God. Life. Death. Resurrection.

Paul's rhetorical question in Romans 6:1 is meant for all of us. We've been so powerfully delivered from our slavery to sin, so why would we want to keep wallowing in it? The story of the prodigal son serves as a great reminder here. When he came back to the father after his long and painful journey and experienced extravagant grace, restoration in the family, and a celebration fit for kings, I cannot imagine him daydreaming with longing about his time feeding pigs while he starved. He was so wonderfully welcomed that he surely couldn't help but begin to develop amnesia about what went on "back there." Certainly, he wouldn't spend long hours thinking about it. No! He had been set free from all that because of his father's love.

We live in a similar scenario. Our Father has welcomed us to himself, gracing us without measure, restoring us into his family, and throwing a kingdom party. That deliverance informs our gratitude, and it should serve to give us amnesia about our past life of sin—not so much that we don't remember it, but that we don't look back on it longingly. We have died to that life, and now, as in baptism, we are raised to a pristine future.

Father, help me remember the story of the prodigal son feeding pigs when I look back longingly on my life entrapped by sin. Instead, give me amnesia about the glory of sin so I can fix my gaze on you and not on my past. I realize that baptism symbolizes what's happened in my heart. I have died to sin. You have resurrected a new life for me. And now I live in light of that. Keep that reality top of mind for me today. Amen.

Day 32

Read Romans 6:5-11

We know that our old sinful selves were crucified with
Christ so that sin might lose its power in our lives.
We are no longer slaves to sin. For when we died with
Christ we were set free from the power of sin.

ROMANS 6:6-7

o you hear echoes of Paul's other words in this verse? Galatians 2:20 reminds us, "My old self has been crucified with Christ. It is no longer I who live, but Christ lives in me. So I live in this earthly body by trusting in the Son of God, who loved me and gave himself for me." Crucifixion ends in death, but resurrection means life. That old self has now died, thanks to the regenerating work of Christ.

It is true, we were enslaved to sin prior to our encounter with Christ. The Greek word used for slavery in Romans 6:6 is *douleuo,* which simply means to be subject to, to be enslaved, or to obey. You may hear echoes of the more familiar Greek word, *doulos,* meaning servant. Later in this narrative, we'll see Paul moving us from being enslaved to sin to being a servant of righteousness—two very different natures.

Before Jesus's rescue, we could not help but sin. It was our very nature, and we obeyed it as if it were our harsh master. But after Jesus, our allegiance shifted, and we now have the option to naturally serve the risen Christ, who can never die again. Before, we were indentured to a defeated enemy of God, Satan, the father of lies. But now in freedom, we serve a powerful King who reigns forever and ever. This doesn't mean we never sin, but it does mean we have a choice not to.

Although there is enslavement language in reference to our new life, the nature of our servitude has changed. Why? Because Jesus now carries our burdens. "Jesus said, 'Come to me, all of you who are weary and carry heavy burdens, and I will give you rest. Take my yoke upon you. Let me teach you, because I am humble and gentle at heart, and you will find rest for your souls. For my yoke is easy to bear, and the burden I give you is light'" (Matthew 11:28-30).

You have moved from harsh slavery to a burden-bearing relationship. From darkness to light. From fear to hope. This is good news!

Father, I want to take some time today to remember what it was like living under sin's tyranny. Sometimes I forget just how miserable that was. Today I choose again to worship, serve, and love you. Right now, I give you all my burdens. They've weighed me down. Thank you that Jesus carries them for me, that he is a gentle Savior who loves and shepherds me well. Amen.

Day 33

Read Romans 6:12-14

Do not let any part of your body become an instrument of evil to serve sin. Instead, give yourselves completely to God, for you were dead, but now you have new life. So use your whole body as an instrument to do what is right for the glory of God.

ROMANS 6:13

Throughout the book of Romans, we see this idea of God requiring us to surrender our bodies to him (most famously in Romans 12:1). Why do you think this is?

Our bodies are the home of the Holy Spirit. But Paul brings that concept even further by declaring that our bodies are the Spirit's temple: "Don't you realize that your body is the temple of the Holy Spirit, who lives in you and was given to you by God? You do not belong to yourself, for God bought you with a high price. So you must honor God with your body" (1 Corinthians 6:19-20).

What we do with our bodies matters. How we live our lives matters. And in light of all that, surrender matters.

Paul uses the word *hoplon* (instrument) in Romans 6:13. It literally means a weapon to wage war. Because there is a spiritual battle all around us, this makes the passage about our bodies even more poignant. What we decide to do with our bodies determines whose side of the spiritual war we are on. If we constantly violate the commandments of God (spoken sins, sexual sins, gluttony of any type, idolatry), we are giving the enemy of our souls a foothold. In Ephesians

4:25-28, we see that how we use our words does just that: "Stop tell-ing lies. Let us tell our neighbors the truth, for we are all parts of the same body. And 'don't sin by letting anger control you.' Don't let the sun go down while you are still angry, for anger gives a foothold to the devil. If you are a thief, quit stealing. Instead, use your hands for good hard work, and then give generously to others in need." Paul affirms that not surrendering our whole lives, including our tongues, leads to a strengthened foothold for Satan. But Paul goes on to give counsel about what we should do instead: Our hands should now work hard and be generous.

How can we do that? By recognizing our surrender is a right response to the generosity of God. Today is a perfect day to surrender. It's a perfect moment to confess what we're ashamed of. It's a perfect time to ask God to transfer us from doing or saying things that make us embarrassed to doing or saying things that represent hard work and Spirit-fueled generosity.

> *Father, I choose today to surrender my body. My mind has entertained impure thoughts. My eyes have stayed too long on sights they shouldn't have. My mouth has destroyed oth-ers. My hands have been swift to gain possessions for myself rather than others. My feet have taken me places I'd rather not have gone. So I'm getting on my knees and surrendering my body to you again. I can't live this life on my own terms, in my own strength. No, I need your Spirit to invigorate me, giving me words and actions that benefit others. Amen.*

Day 34

Read Romans 6:15-19

*Since God's grace has set us free from the law, does that mean
we can go on sinning? Of course not! Don't you realize that you
become the slave of whatever you choose to obey? You can be a
slave to sin, which leads to death, or you can choose to obey God,
which leads to righteous living.*

ROMANS 6:15-16

The phrase that keeps jumping out at me as I read this passage is "Of course not!" I wanted to know just how strongly this exclamation was in the original Greek. The term is actually two words, *me genoito. Me* is a negative particle; in other words, it strongly negates what follows it. The verb *ginomai* (conjugated *genoito* here) means to happen or become. So if you put those two together, you get something along the lines of "May it never happen." Unfortunately, this feels pretty light and doesn't convey the vigor with which Paul uses it. In the New Living Translation, we see a stronger rendering: "Of course not!" (with an exclamation point to show the reader that this is a definitive line in the sand, a rigorous no).

Genoito can also mean *may it be.*[12] So to negate it makes the declaration, "May it *never* be!" This is closer to the rigor of the text—which essentially means absolutely not, or by no means! What Paul is saying here is a counterargument to the ridiculousness of thinking that license (doing whatever you want to do, whenever you want to do it, then slapping grace on it like an ill-fitting bandage) is something we should choose in light of grace. The connotation is that since we've been freed from the bondage of sin, how can we go back to the muck and mire of it? Why would we want to? We've been set free, so why go back to the shackles of sin's slavery?

The solution is to switch your allegiance. When sin knocks on your mind and heart, enticing you to egregious rebellion, then whispers, "It's okay; do whatever you want. God wants you to be happy. Grace will cover it," it's time to say, "May it *never* be! I am a child of God, set free from sin. Why would I enslave myself to sin when I can submit myself to the One who secured my freedom?"

Father, may it never be that I willingly bow down to sin's control in my life. Please forgive me for treating your grace like a bauble instead of the jewel that it is. May it never be that I choose sin over you. I want to live my life in a way that makes you smile. I want to be set free from the sin that strives to control my thoughts and behaviors. And to do that? I need you. Every day. Every hour. Every minute. Amen.

Day 35

Read Romans 6:20-23

You are now ashamed of the things you used to do, things that end in eternal doom. But now you are free from the power of sin and have become slaves of God. Now you do those things that lead to holiness and result in eternal life.

ROMANS 6:21-22

There are two yous: the you before Christ and the you after Christ. The you before Christ did things you regret today. But because of the blood of Jesus shed on behalf of the entirety of the human race, you are set free from those things—even the regrets. The old you has been crucified alongside Christ, and the new you is indwelled with the Holy Spirit. This new you longs to do what is right. You now desire to be holy, and you look with joyful anticipation for the unfolding of God's dynamic kingdom.

When we examine the payoff for our sin had we remained in it and not sought Jesus for help through repentance, it's not a pretty picture. The word Paul uses in Romans 6:21 is *thanatos,* a dark word. It's "derived from *thnḗskō,* 'to die'—physical or spiritual *death*; (figuratively) separation from the life (salvation) of God forever by dying without first experiencing *death to self* to receive His gift of salvation."[13] This stark word means eternal separation. It's the state of our souls prior to Christ, and it is the destiny of those who don't yet call Jesus Lord. In light of that, we can do two things: thank God for such an amazing deliverance from death to life and pray fervently for those who don't yet know him.

Wages are earned. They are deserved. And when we wallow in a life of sin apart from God, we will earn this death. The word used in Romans 6:23 is "*opsónion* (from *opson*, 'meat' and *onemoai*, 'purchase')." It literally means to pay for provisions.[14] Think of that. Our provisions (what should supply life) from a life of sin are like poison.

The best word in verse 23, however, is not *death* or *wages*. It is *but*. Yes, this was true of us. Yes, our pay for a sin-entrenched life was poison and death. *But*, because of Jesus, we have a free gift, something gloriously unearned and undeserved—new life in Christ. Let's thank him for that.

> *Father, I'm amazed at what you did by sending Jesus to die for my sins. Help me live in gratitude for all he's done. I am no longer earning poison wages. Instead, you've graced me with freedom and deliverance. I pray for all those friends and family members whose wages (currently) are death. Would you beckon them to yourself today? Would you rescue them? I pray they'd bow the knee, repent, and turn to you—the giver of life. Amen.*

ROMANS 1

Emancipation from sin, death, lies, and futility is a glorious thing. Christ's crucifixion and resurrection have inaugurated glorious freedom.

WILD LOVE

I do what I shouldn't
I don't do as I should
I'm mired in sinfulness
Choosing me over you

But you died for my weakness
You wore all my shame
My sin deserves justice
So you paid my great debt

CHORUS
Oh, your wild love
That sets me free
From the tyranny of fear
Crucified, you bled
On that crooked tree
Once far, now you have come near
It's your law I have broken
I'm as guilty as sin
I have chased heartaches
Believing life springs from them

But you donned my weakness
You limped the same human path
As an empathetic Savior
Who has borne my regret

BRIDGE
Deliver me from selfishness
Deliver me from me
Deliver me from helplessness
Deliver me from greed
Deliver me from recklessness
I choose to bend the knee
Before the throne
Of the wild One
Whose love has rescued me

Day 36

Read Romans 7:1-3

*Dear brothers and sisters—you who are familiar
with the law—don't you know that the law applies
only while a person is living?*

ROMANS 7:1

Marriage is binding—a powerful representation of the covenant God has with his church. But if a spouse passes away, the remaining widow or widower is free to marry again, not charged with committing adultery. All this is obvious, but Paul is using this example to demonstrate the dynamic transformation that happens to us when we understand our new relationship with the law. In the next passage, we'll see Paul's behind-the-scenes logic of what it means to die to the law, and why that is important.

But right now, I want to focus on the tone in which Paul is addressing the church here. We sometimes get the impression Paul is harsh. We see this accusation in 2 Corinthians 10:9-11 when Paul writes, "I'm not trying to frighten you by my letters. For some say, 'Paul's letters are demanding and forceful, but in person he is weak, and his speeches are worthless!' Those people should realize that our actions when we arrive in person will be as forceful as what we say in our letters from far away." In terms of calling out sin and speaking the truth, Paul is unwavering.

But then we see his compassion as well. We'll see in Romans 9:2-3 just how much he loves those he's writing to: "My heart is filled with

bitter sorrow and unending grief for my people, my Jewish brothers and sisters. I would be willing to be forever cursed—cut off from
Christ!—if that would save them." Paul's first affection, his reason for
living, is Jesus Christ. And yet he is willing to be severed from him for
the sake of his countrymen, those he loves, something he relays when
he calls his audience "dear brothers and sisters" in Romans 7:1.

This is the kind of affection we must have for those in our lives,
that our love would compel us to speak the truth, pray with vigor, and
see all humanity as brothers and sisters, dearly loved of the One who
created them. We should long to see people set free from the law that
ensnares them so they can truly encounter the risen Christ. We should
emulate God's kindness toward everyone, but also represent his heart,
which is to see everyone come to know him. Peter reminds us of this
great, great heart: "The Lord isn't really being slow about his promise, as some people think. No, he is being patient for your sake. He
does not want anyone to be destroyed, but wants everyone to repent"
(2 Peter 3:9). Let's pray for that today.

*Father, help me see the people in my life as family members
even before they're part of your family. Empower my brothers and sisters to come to that great understanding—that
they are in need of a Savior; that the law cannot save them,
only condemn them; and that living life for themselves in
their own strength will only result in rancor and stress. Oh,
how I long to see them meet you. Please save my loved ones.
Amen.*

Day 31

Read Romans 7:4-6

My dear brothers and sisters, this is the point: You died to the power of the law when you died with Christ. And now you are united with the one who was raised from the dead. As a result, we can produce a harvest of good deeds for God.

Romans 7:4

A good exercise in reading and studying the book of Romans is to highlight or circle words that commonly repeat. For example, I drew a pyramid (pointing heavenward) to highlight the words *life* and *live* and *alive* and an inverted triangle (pointing toward the earth) to highlight *death* and *died.* We'll see these in abundance throughout Romans, but particularly in this passage. We see this life-and-death battle clearly depicted.

Similar to the freedom a wife has to remarry after the tragedy of her husband's death, once our old nature is crucified, we are free to marry (or be joined to) the One who rose again—Jesus Christ. Baptism, as we've studied before, is a physical picture of this paradox. We die with Jesus, and then we live with him in newness of life.

Prior to this choice to follow Jesus down this death-then-life road, the best we could hope for was death. Our deeds were dead. Our hopes were dead. Our hearts were deadened to the goodness of God. Our outlook? Bleak.

But now? Life, life, life. Jesus promised this when he highlighted the life-and-death battle we've experienced: "The thief comes only to steal and kill and destroy. I came that they may have life and have it abundantly" (John 10:10 ESV). Once we were enslaved to the world, Satan, and our sin nature, which resulted in being stolen from, dying, and experiencing destruction. But now—blessed now!—we walk in abundance, anchored to the Author of life.

When death to self happens, we experience the great exchange. Our sin nature is conquered through Jesus, and our emptiness is replaced by the Holy Spirit, a constant companion who not only fills our hearts with peace and joy, but who stays with us through life's storms. He gives us the uncanny ability (one we didn't previously have) to say no to temptation. He comforts us when life is difficult (and it will be). When others leave us, or we experience loss and heartache, the Spirit is our ever-present friend.

In light of all this, all we can do is humbly rejoice. What an outrageously amazing gift! From death to life. From feeling abandoned to befriended. From powerless to empowered.

> *Father, I appreciate you. In fact, the word appreciate seems way too small. I want to spend my life praising you for what you've done. You rescued me from my death-bent ways. You replaced my propensity to sin with the Spirit, who empowers me to live with joy. You are always with me. Your pursuit of me humbles me, gives me peace, and renews my vision for today. I love you. Amen.*

Day 38

Read Romans 7:7-13

It was the law that showed me my sin. I would never have
known that coveting is wrong if the law had not said,
"You must not covet." But sin used this command to
arouse all kinds of covetous desires within me!

ROMANS 7:7-8

We will see Paul revisit the sin of coveting later in Romans 13:9. So often we gloss over this sin without giving it much thought. Here's what it is: "The coveting which the Tenth Commandment condemns is the desire to have something which one does not have, or which one does not think he or she has enough of. In brief, coveting wants more. It is not content with what it already has, no matter how much that might be."[15] So to covet means to want something you can't have so much that it consumes your affections, hurts other people, and wounds your relationship with God. In short, it's a big deal.

How do we get rid of this insidious sin in our lives? We give thanks to the One who rescued us from this sin. The more we focus on God, then serve others in humility, the less we think about the portions of the kingdom that are not ours. The less we poke around social media and instead socialize with humans in our actual lives, the better off we are in our battle with coveting.

If you're hurting today because you can't keep your mind off that one thing or person or trait or goal that you seemingly can never have, take heart. There is a cure. It's called gratitude. It's called listing what you're thankful for right now and taking a moment (or two or ten thousand) to thank God for all he has done and is doing. Trace his handiwork in your life, friend. Seek to see his work. Instead of acting adolescently, whining that God isn't giving you everything you want, be mature and grateful that he is a good Father who sometimes doesn't give us what we think we deserve.

> *Father, I don't want to covet what other people have. I don't want to spend my life fretting about it, conniving to get it, or lamenting that I don't have it. I realize that in myself I can't conquer this sin; I need your help. I choose today to live in gratitude. I'm grateful for you. I'm grateful for the life you've given me, the people in my life, the hope you've instilled in me because of the life, death, and resurrection of your Son. Help me rest there today. Amen.*

Day 39

Read Romans 7:14-23

*I have discovered this principle of life—that when I want
to do what is right, I inevitably do what is wrong. I love
God's law with all my heart. But there is another power
within me that is at war with my mind. This power makes
me a slave to the sin that is still within me.*

ROMANS 7:21-23

There are varying opinions about the time frame Paul is referring to when he speaks of his struggle against sin here. After reading this passage dozens of times in preparation for this book, I'm convinced he is referring to the gravity of his past struggle before Christ. Before the Damascus road, he imprisoned and voted to execute Christians (Acts 26:9-11). He harmed the cause of Christ and tried his best to annihilate the church. Not only was he enslaved to his sin nature, but he also persecuted the church.

We will see in Romans 8 that Jesus is the One who delivered Paul from this sin nature. Now, does that mean Paul became sinless and never struggled from that point on? No. But his struggle was entirely different. Prior to Christ, he couldn't help but sin all the time. He had no way to resist temptation, nor could he even want to. But after Christ, he received the Holy Spirit, who empowered him to live a new life. The nature of the struggle changed significantly.

We were once enslaved to sin, but now we're set free from its power. In this world, we will experience temptation. We will disappoint a holy God, and we'll grow frustrated at ourselves when we can't seem to conquer a particular sin in our lives. But we face this struggle with the help of the Spirit, our constant companion. Before, we could sin without conscience, but now we have the conviction of the Spirit to steer us back to the Father. Before, we didn't even realize we lived self-absorbed lives, but now the Spirit inaugurates compassion in our hearts. Before, we were enslaved to doing wrong, but now we are slaves of righteousness.

When you battle sin in your current life, remember this: The battle has already been won. Your sin nature has been fatally wounded, and God has given you the Spirit to help you choose a life that makes God smile. The wrestling is over. Forgiveness is yours the moment you repent of your current sin. You can have newness of life right now—all because of the victory Christ won on the cross.

> *Father, I confess my current sins to you. I need forgiveness. I need hope. I need to turn away from what I thought would satisfy me and turn toward you, the One who truly does satiate my thirst. Thank you that the battle is already won, that I don't have to be enslaved to sin like I was before I met you. Remind me of the Spirit's presence in my life today. I don't want to quench his work in my life. Instead, I want to embrace his comfort and power. Amen.*

Day 40

Read Romans 7:24-25

Oh, what a miserable person I am! Who will free me from this life that is dominated by sin and death? Thank God! The answer is in Jesus Christ our Lord.

ROMANS 7:24-25

You've probably heard "Jesus is the answer." And in the case of your sin problem (which is better stated as "a sin catastrophe"), he truly is. No one else can free you from your sin. Not even you. You are powerless to change your nature. You cannot choose what is right without Jesus Christ. A life dominated by sin and darkness is the common state of all who don't (yet) know him.

Can you hear the desperation in Paul's voice? The utter frustration? Prior to the road-to-Damascus experience, he had "everything" he wanted. He was well respected, a Pharisee of Pharisees, an expert in the law. But none of that knowledge or stature empowered him to live a life worthy of God. None of that prestige gave him the strength he needed to overcome his minute-by-minute propensity for sin.

"Enslaved" is the best way to describe this state. Sin is a terribly relentless master, and it forces all humanity to obey its lusts, infecting us down to the marrow of our will and desire.

What are we to do? And how are we to live now?

To do? Surrender to Jesus. Believe in him who lived a perfect life, died a substitutionary death in our place, made us right with God, and rose again, defeating sin, death, and the devil once and for all.

How to live now? In utter gratitude, because Jesus took care of it all. We may try to live a perfect life in our own strength based on personal grit, but what God asks of us, besides surrender, is faith in his goodness, his availability, his power, his strength, his Spirit. We must come to the end of ourselves, all that wasted effort trying to be good, and bow humbly before the cross.

The good that comes after that kneeling is the result of the Spirit's invigorated life within us, a life full of thankfulness and joy. Jesus did what we couldn't. He lived the way we failed to. He rescued us from the sin that so easily entangled us. He performed a mighty resurrection in our hearts after our surrender. And because of all that, our lives are best lived with renewed minds, cleansed hearts, and the constant presence of the One who secured our freedom.

Father, I go back today to the day I asked Jesus to be the Lord of my life. Help me return to that place of first love, where I lived overwhelmed with your goodness. Thank you for rescuing me from the enslavement of sin. Thank you for providing a way for me to be right with you. Thank you that I came to the end of myself so I could reach for you. Amen.

ROMANS 8

*I've heard Romans 8:28 shared as a heartless cliché.
This song pushes against that ripped-from-context platitude.
Life is harder, more nuanced. Yes, God works things for good,
but that doesn't mean we don't struggle and suffer
in this sin-darkened world.*

WHERE WERE YOU?

Lord, where were you when the darkness crashed over
Like wave upon wave on the sea?
Lord, where were you when my breath, it was stolen,
While anxiety ripped life from me?
I know all the words I should joyfully say
Words of your plan, but they all sound cliché
I sit still in the pain, longing for brand-new light
Lord, where was your hand when I groveled at night?

CHORUS

In the midst of the drowning
I grabbed for your hand
That bled to the touch
You reached and you rescued
Then healed my heart
Then called me your beloved
The one whom you love

Lord, where were you when I suffered injustice
For days turned to weeks, then to years?
Lord, where were you when my spirit was groaning
While my fear added fuel to my tears?
I know I should trust in your sovereign hand
While the story unfolds, but not how I planned
I fret in the dark, hoping for weighted glory
Lord, where were you when I lost every mooring?

BRIDGE

You shift pain into hope
Shower love as I falter
Nothing can separate me from you
You shift worry to worship
Grant me holy perspective
I'm your child; you're my Abba; that's the truth

Day 41

Read Romans 8:1-4

*Now there is no condemnation for those who belong to
Christ Jesus. And because you belong to him, the power
of the life-giving Spirit has freed you from the
power of sin that leads to death.*

ROMANS 8:1-2

If you picture a courtroom with a defendant, an attorney, a judge, a victim, and a jury, you can appreciate the point of this word. Condemnation is the just sentence handed down after guilt has been determined. In other words, we have been declared guilty by a righteous Judge, and our penalty will be deserved—and it will match the crime.

But Jesus.

Jesus entered the holy law court as the defendant. He stood in our place, receiving the penalty we deserved by being sinners—which is death. Crucified and buried, he superseded the entire system by rising from the dead. And now, as we place our faith in that completed work, we can walk this earth freely, emancipated from sin's rightful penalty.

The law demanded justice. It could not empower us to obey it. It only showed us how far we fell short. It was not alive, not able to change a heart. And so, as we hung our heads in the dire sadness of the courtroom, we were without excuse and without hope.

Jesus did what the law could not do. He did what *we* could not do.

This is why he is the King of kings and the Lord of lords, and at his name, every knee will bow in heaven and on earth (Philippians

2:10). That is why we place our faith in him—our rescuer, Savior, healer, Redeemer.

And if that feels like far too much good news, there is more. Not only did he die for us, take our penalty, and rise in the aftermath, but he also sent his Spirit into our hearts. Where the Spirit fell upon others sporadically throughout the Old Testament, he now takes up permanent residence in our hearts. We are never, ever alone. He will never leave nor forsake us.

> *Father, I'm stunned to silence. I deserve the penalty, but Jesus didn't. Yet he loved me enough to take my place in the courtroom. How can I thank you? I'm not only set free from sin's menacing power, but you've given me your Spirit to be with me forever, a constant companion who gives me the strength to follow you. I love you. I need you. I adore you. I worship you. Amen.*

Day 42

Read Romans 8:5-11

Those who are dominated by the sinful nature think about sinful things, but those who are controlled by the Holy Spirit think about things that please the Spirit. So letting your sinful nature control your mind leads to death. But letting the Spirit control your mind leads to life and peace.

ROMANS 8:5-6

Throughout Romans, Paul is consistent with his theme of the Spirit living within us, but particularly here. What reveals our Christianity? The Spirit abiding (making his home) in us. We are the receptacles of his glorious, powerful presence. Elsewhere, Paul refers to our bodies as the Spirit's temple (see 1 Corinthians 6:19-20). Later, we'll see this correlation with how we should live in our bodies in Romans 12, but for now, let's remember the simple, yet paradoxical truth that we are homes for the Holy Spirit.

And in that symbiotic relationship, control is transferred. We move from being controlled by our sinful nature, where we're rendered helpless in our fight against sin, toward surrendering control to the Spirit. We are no longer dominated by sinful thoughts and actions, but now we spend our lives growing in our ability to hear the Spirit speak words of encouragement in and through us. Not only that, but the Spirit also gives us life—the kind of abundant life we longed for when we were enslaved to sin.

Blaise Pascal wrote about our empty lives before Christ (*Pensées*

7.425.5): "What is it, then, that this desire and this inability proclaim to us, but that there was once in man a true happiness of which there now remain to him only the mark and empty trace, which he in vain tries to fill from all his surroundings, seeking from things absent the help he does not obtain in things present? But these are all inadequate, because the infinite abyss can only be filled by an infinite and immutable object, that is to say, only by God Himself."

What a beautiful truth. We were once homeless wanderers, filling our lives with anything but God, and now we're not only filled, but we become the very home of the Spirit.

> *Father, I confess there were many days when I chased after everything but you. I was empty, longing to fill the insatiable hole in my heart. Thank you for rescuing me, then sending the Spirit to make a home in my heart. I am filled! I am alive! I have abundance! All because of your outrageous generosity. Amen.*

Day 43

Read Romans 8:12-17

You have not received a spirit that makes you fearful slaves.
Instead, you received God's Spirit when he adopted you as his
own children. Now we call him, "Abba, Father."

ROMANS 8:15

Outsider to insider. Orphan to adopted. Enslaved to free. What glorious, powerful promises our God gives us in these verses. This is the miracle of the gospel, the reason we sing, the hope of the world. It's why we proclaim the excellencies of Jesus. It's why we cannot help but sing praises and bend our knees and cry out in thanksgiving.

When Paul talks about "fearful slaves," the implication in the Greek is having the same kind of manner and mind-set as one who has lived in the lifelong harassment and abuse of slavery. That's what the law and our sin have been for us. They tied us up, taunted and tainted us, and gave us no way to be successful under their cruel tutelage. In short, we lived under the terrorism of an entirely unwinnable situation.

Contrast this to the meaning of *adoption*. The Greek refers to a slave who has been given the full rights of a son, moving from enslaved outsider to rightful heir. What a change in situation—from pauper to son. It is a legal term, used within Greek culture to give right standing to a slave, removing that painful moniker and replacing it with sonship.

The response we have to the God who inaugurated this adoption is to call him Daddy, or *Abba,* the Aramaic word for *father*. It's a term of endearment, one used by children to sweetly grab the attention of their father. "Daddy! Daddy! See me! Pick me up!"

Now that we are legally adopted through the sacrifice of Jesus, we have this holy privilege of calling the God of the universe our daddy. It's uncanny. It's beautiful. It's hard to believe. But it's true. In light of that, our simple response today is worship.

> *Daddy, Abba, thank you. Thank you that my status as an adopted child of yours cannot be reversed. I have been bought with a price, and I cannot be unbought. Thank you for setting me free from the terrorism of the law and my own battle against sin. Thank you for calling me your beloved child. My response today is to worship you. Amen.*

Day 44

Read Romans 8:18-25

We know that all creation has been groaning as in the pains of childbirth right up to the present time. And we believers also groan, even though we have the Holy Spirit within us as a foretaste of future glory, for we long for our bodies to be released from sin and suffering. We, too, wait with eager hope for the day when God will give us our full rights as his adopted children, including the new bodies he has promised us.

ROMANS 8:22-23

We see in Paul's other writings this powerful principle that the Spirit within us is our down payment for our new life awaiting us on heaven's shores. In Ephesians 1:14, he says, "The Spirit is God's guarantee that he will give us the inheritance he promised and that he has purchased us to be his own people. He did this so we would praise and glorify him." In 2 Corinthians 1:22, he reminds us that God "has identified us as his own by placing the Holy Spirit in our hearts as the first installment that guarantees everything he has promised us."

What will happen will be more glorious than what has happened. His kingdom is here, and it is coming—the great conundrum of the now and the not yet. You see this also praised by Paul in 2 Corinthians 5:1-5:

> We know that when this earthly tent we live in is taken down (that is, when we die and leave this earthly body), we will have a house in heaven, an eternal body made for us

by God himself and not by human hands. We grow weary in our present bodies, and we long to put on our heavenly bodies like new clothing. For we will put on heavenly bodies; we will not be spirits without bodies. While we live in these earthly bodies, we groan and sigh, but it's not that we want to die and get rid of these bodies that clothe us. Rather, we want to put on our new bodies so that these dying bodies will be swallowed up by life. God himself has prepared us for this, and as a guarantee he has given us his Holy Spirit.

Friend, this is foundational. Heaven is real. The Spirit within you is the guarantee, the down payment on the loan that will be fulfilled. The precious and powerful blood of Christ has bought this reality. Your occupation here on earth is to remember that you were created, as Randy Alcorn has said, for a person and a place—that person is Jesus, and that place is heaven.[16] Don't lose hope. Don't give up. One day all will be made right.

Father, thank you for giving me the Holy Spirit as a deposit on the kind of real estate that can never be foreclosed upon—a home where righteousness dwells and all my tears are wiped away. Help me live in light of this great promise. I don't want to lose heart today, but to concentrate fully on what you will do. Amen.

Day 45

Read Romans 8:26-30

*The Holy Spirit helps us in our weakness. For example,
we don't know what God wants us to pray for. But the Holy
Spirit prays for us with groanings that cannot be expressed in
words. And the Father who knows all hearts knows what the
Spirit is saying, for the Spirit pleads for us believers
in harmony with God's own will.*

ROMANS 8:26-27

The Holy Spirit within us gives us life. He empowers our choices, is our steady companion day in and day out, and intercedes when we cannot. He is God the Father's gift to us, but so often we relegate him to a faceless force, grossly misunderstanding the third person of the Trinity. The Spirit is wholly God, indwelling us. The Spirit was there at creation, hovering over the waters. He was present throughout the Old Testament, lighting on some, leaving others. He proclaimed the sonship of Jesus at his baptism, and he was the one who fell powerfully on the new believers at Pentecost, igniting new languages, miracles, and healing.

And he is within you.

As I write those words, it's almost too much to consider. The God of the cosmos comes so near that he indwells our fissures and bloodstream, our heart and heartache, our mind and mannerisms. And when we are broken, he shines all the more by interceding for us. He prays for us according to the will of God, even when we cannot discern it. He intervenes, gives voice to the words we cannot utter.

Through the Holy Spirit, we glimpse eternity. Through the Holy Spirit, we participate in the great uncovering of the will of God, as he works everything out in the end for his glory. And that working out is purposeful. It's beautifully calculated. What is his will? It's for us to be conformed into the image of Jesus Christ. We start that journey through justification, being made wholly right before God through Christ. We continue it alongside our brothers and sisters in community, a body of believers who are called out. And we finish working out our salvation empowered by the Spirit. All this results in glory—a word that comes from *doxa,* which has many powerful connotations. It means weighty, heavy, having worth, full of splendor. Because of the Spirit in our lives, we cannot help but feel the weight of his worth, and this informs our own worth.

> *Father, thank you for giving me the Spirit. Thank you that the Spirit within me intercedes when my words have left me. I'm humbled by this, and oh so grateful. Thank you for working everything out for my good, for your good, for the good of the kingdom, though I don't always discern it in the moment. Thank you for glory, for weight, for splendor, for worth. You are all those things. I love you. Amen.*

Day 46

Read Romans 8:31-34

Who dares accuse us whom God has chosen for his own? No one—for God himself has given us right standing with himself.

ROMANS 8:33

When you're best friends with the king's son, you have certain rights. And when you're a fellow heir (adopted into the king's family), no one can mess with you. No authority can challenge a king's leadership. No one beneath him can legally usurp his authority. Because he reigns supreme, you can be assured of your safety.

This is the truth of who you are: a child of the King of kings. And that King is *for* you. He secured your newfound position as his child—moving you from pauper to member of the royal family. This truly is wonderful news, a status to wonder about. He gave up his Son so we could be in right relationship with himself—the kind of sacrifice that is difficult to fathom, even after years of pondering it.

And now this Son—Jesus Christ—sits in power at God's right hand. This powerful, almighty, resurrected Savior is also our chief intercessor, intervening and praying on our behalf. This is our royal status in the kingdom of God. It is resolute, fixed. It cannot be changed, as it is backed by the highest royalty, the Creator of everything we see.

You have been chosen to bear fruit for the sake of the One who sent his Son to rescue you. You are his, bought with the blood of Jesus. You are empowered by his Spirit, loved like a child, always interceded for.

Your rescued state is a joyful reality because the very One who could condemn you is actually your Savior, who now lives to intervene on your behalf. While you were once an enemy to the things of God, now you are a privileged insider, well loved and welcomed.

Spend some time today re-preaching this gospel (the Good News) to yourself. It never grows old—your renewed relationship with this amazing God!

Father, from outsider to insider, outcast to beloved, alien to countryman—you have welcomed me into your royal household as your child. I sit in awe of what you've done. I couldn't do this on my own; I'd be an interloper, a thief trying to break into the castle. But you've opened wide the gate, and I'm inside, so very loved by you. "Thank you" doesn't seem enough. Amen.

Day 41

Read Romans 8:35-39

*Can anything ever separate us from Christ's love? Does it
mean he no longer loves us if we have trouble or calamity,
or are persecuted, or hungry, or destitute, or in danger, or
threatened with death? (As the Scriptures say, "For your sake
we are killed every day; we are being slaughtered like sheep.")
No, despite all these things, overwhelming victory is ours
through Christ, who loved us.*

ROMANS 8:35-37

These days, it seems when the gospel is shared, we learn about all
the benefits, which is heartening. While once enemies of God,
we're now brought near. He renews our hearts, gives us a new view on
life, sets us free from the power of sin, and gives us a life of purpose.
But somewhere along the line, we believe only one side of the Good
News—about all the good stuff. We forget that the gospel originated
from a violent crucifixion, and that as we follow in the footsteps of our
Savior, we will also be called upon to die.

So when trials and temptations come our way, as they inevitably
do, we get angry. We may naively think God owes us a happy life from
the moment we were made right with him. But he never promised us
immunity to life's challenges. Instead, he promised his presence. Jesus
said, "I have told you all this so that you may have peace in me. Here
on earth you will have many trials and sorrows. But take heart, because

I have overcome the world" (John 16:33). He did warn us. Trials come, but he will be with us.

That's the difference between the Christ follower going through trials and the person who is without Christ. One has peace and presence, but the other does not. One has connection to the Creator, but the other does not.

Yes, pain will come. But that pain is not an indication that God has left us or no longer loves us. We're promised in these verses that absolutely nothing—not even horrific circumstances—can negate his affection and kindness toward us. Just as we love our children when they walk through pain, our God loves us and wants to walk alongside us when we encounter our own pain.

Father, thank you that nothing separates me from your love—even the trials that seem to come upon me wave after wave. Instead of seeing those circumstances as negations of your love, let me instead seek you in the midst of the pain. I need your peace and presence in my current frustration and worry. Be near. Show me you love me. Help me rest in that today. Amen.

ROMANS 9

While Paul laments his countrymen and friends, longing for them to come home to Christ, I feel that ache as well. I have prodigal friends and family members who pepper my prayer list. I wrote this as a prayer and a song for the prodigals in our lives.

PRODIGAL SONG

I sing on behalf of those far, far from you
Placing them firm in your nail-scarred palms
Surrendering my need for control at your feet
Oh Jesus, they're yours; they're not mine

CHORUS

Increase my faith to imagine them home
Alive, repentant, set free
Don't let me give in to a broken despair
Afraid, yet I am trusting thee

I mourn their long journey to the prodigal lands
Feeling weighed down by their sin-fueled choice
Wondering if I should talk or just listen
Oh Jesus, they're yours; they're not mine

I laugh in strong hope of their grand re-imagining
To the life of the godly and free
Resurrecting from death and their wayward dreaming
Oh Jesus, they're yours; they're not mine

BRIDGE

More than me
You stand waiting
Scanning sin's blank horizon
For a glimpse of the one who is far
Your ring circles a finger
Your robe welcomes them back
To the broken family of grace

Day 48

Read Romans 9:1-5

My heart is filled with bitter sorrow and unending grief for my people, my Jewish brothers and sisters. I would be willing to be forever cursed—cut off from Christ!—if that would save them.

ROMANS 9:2-3

Do you have people in your life who live far from God? Have you agonized over their rebellion? Do you ache when people slander God or seem to think he can't see their actions? Paul feels this similar pain and love, mixed in equal portions. The Jews are his people, the very folks in the lineage of Christ. Their blood coursed through Jesus. His Father had created the covenants they boasted about. Their ceremonies and worship times pointed to him. The temple represented the very presence of God that he embodied. And yet, they missed the Messiah.

Paul must've wondered why he had been privileged to meet Jesus on the road to Damascus—why he, who had been wholly rebellious, experienced radical rescue. Although he spent his adult Christian life ministering to those outside the Jewish faith (Gentiles), his heart still longed to see his brothers and sisters come into the full realization of what it meant to be loved by God.

Paul's heart for his people is evident in his outcry. His longing is so severe that he considers the utmost penalty—being severed from the presence of Christ—for the sake of his countrymen. Later, we read just how important the nearness of Jesus means to Paul. He writes, "To me, living means living for Christ, and dying is even better. But if I live, I can do more fruitful work for Christ. So I really don't know which is better. I'm torn between two desires: I long to go and be with Christ, which would be far better for me. But for your sakes, it is better that I continue to live" (Philippians 1:21-24). Here, too, we see his deep longing for all people—not only his Jewish brothers and sisters—to know this same Jesus who has utterly changed his life.

You may be aching inside for those you love who don't yet know Christ. Like Paul, you long to see them be redeemed. Continue to press on. Continue to experience the amazing presence of Jesus. Pray like crazy. And entrust them to the God who loves to save the lost—even someone so once-enemy-like as the apostle Paul.

> *Father, today I lift up those I know who don't yet know you. Would you chase them today? Would you show them who you are? Help me be mindful of them when I'm awake at night or going throughout my day. I want to pray for them often. Thank you that you rescued those who were exceptionally far from you—even the apostle Paul, who called himself the chief of sinners. If you could radically save him, I choose to have hope that you can save my loved ones. Amen.*

Day 49

Read Romans 9:6-9

Abraham's physical descendants are not necessarily children of God. Only the children of the promise are considered to be Abraham's children.

ROMANS 9:8

R omans 9 is hard for me to grasp because I cannot wrap my mind around the doctrine of election. I used to see that as a detriment, but now I embrace the ambiguity because I've come into a deeper understanding of God's character. I don't understand every nuance of Calvinism or Arminian thought, but I love Jesus, and I live in the tension of those views.

The tension is broken by the unknowable, otherly God. His ways, we'll see later, are higher than ours. His plans? Deeper and wider and wiser than I can fathom. How he weaves all our stories into a grand redemptive narrative, I cannot begin to discern. That is because I have a small mind in comparison to his vast intelligence.

In fact, the longer I walk this earth, the more I realize what I do not know. Yet the more I see God's confounding faithfulness, the more I learn to trust him. He is glorious. He is fatherly. He is powerful. He is a conundrum. He is beautiful. And I am his.

You don't have to have all your theological ideations dotted and your ontological arguments crossed. What you need is simple obedience. Hear God's heart in the Scriptures, then obey. Follow in the footsteps of Jesus, even in the paradox. Trust the hand of the One who formed you in darkness. Entrust your doubts to him. He will not push you away for having real concerns about the way he works. Besides, he already knows your struggles and wants to continue in relationship with you through them.

Rejoice today that you are a child of promise, chosen by him, sacrificed for, wholly accepted. This is good news. As you obey, your trust grows. And as your trust grows, your peace multiplies—even in your wrangling.

> *Father, I'm simply grateful that you've chosen me to be your child. I don't understand the intricacies of your ways or the way your plan unfolds in this world. But I do know that those who follow you are dearly loved, won over by your pursuit. I pray for those who don't yet know you, that you would pursue them today with vigor. Amen.*

Day 50

Read Romans 9:10-16

This message shows that God chooses people according to his own purposes; he calls people, but not according to their good or bad works.

ROMANS 9:11-12

G od calls us not because of our good works, but because of his plan and will. We do not merit the call—it's the grand merit of Jesus who died in our place that grants us this privilege of followership. In short, this life of faith is not about us. It's about him.

But so often we make it about us. We center our worship songs around our bravery, our prowess, our being graced. Our vertical singing has shifted horizontally, where we praise the created more than we elevate the Creator. But he is the reason we exist. He is the Creator of all—the fashioner of galaxies, DNA, prehensile tails, a baby's yelp, ripe peaches, friendship. Not only that, but he holds the entire cosmos together and will one day judge every person justly. He is the Creator, and this is not a democracy; he is the ruler, and we are the joyfully ruled.

Even our salvation has nothing to do with us. We could not do enough good deeds to gain entrance into his kingdom. We could try a myriad of holiness gymnastics to make it work, but ultimately, we would always fall short. The way, we hear from the mouth of Jesus, is narrow, and the only way to truly be in relationship with our heavenly

Father is to pass through the narrow gate of Jesus—who is also the truth and the life (see John 14:6).

As humanity, we bear the scars and marks of sin. We inherited its downfalls. We walked in its insidiousness, enslaved. We were sinners in desperate need of rescue, but no matter how many ladders we made or buildings we erected skyward (I'm thinking of Babel), our hands could not grasp eternity.

Which is why God rescued us—sending his Son to do what we could never do for ourselves. He lived sinlessly in a sin-rippled world. He battled the enemy of our souls. He pushed against the spiritually proud who thought they had "made it" into the kingdom. He loved like crazy all the folks who felt the weight of the impossibility of perfection. He waded into our world, plucked us from drowning waves, and rescued us.

That's why he gets all the glory from our story. He is the rescuer, we the rescued. This gospel is about him, not us.

Father, forgive me for getting caught up in myself and worshipping my wants over your glory. You have done it all. You have made a narrow way. You have provided everything I need for life and godliness. You are everything, and everything is for you. I bow down today. I subjugate my heart before you, singing worship songs of your might and power. Oh, how amazing you are. Amen.

Day 51

Read Romans 9:17-24

When a potter makes jars out of clay, doesn't he have a right to use the same lump of clay to make one jar for decoration and another to throw garbage into? In the same way, even though God has the right to show his anger and his power, he is very patient with those on whom his anger falls, who are destined for destruction. He does this to make the riches of his glory shine even brighter on those to whom he shows mercy, who were prepared in advance for glory.

ROMANS 9:21-23

What a powerful truth: We are prepared in advance for glory. Like a coach prepares an athlete for competition, God prepares us for glory as we participate in his kingdom. In that crucible of preparation, he fashions us like a potter throws a pot. We see that language throughout the Bible, notably in Isaiah 64:8: "O LORD, you are our Father. We are the clay, and you are the potter. We all are formed by your hand." Later, we see the prophet Jeremiah interacting with the Lord about this same idea.

> I did as he told me and found the potter working at his wheel. But the jar he was making did not turn out as he had hoped, so he crushed it into a lump of clay again and started over. Then the LORD gave me this message: "O Israel, can I not do to you as this potter has done to his

clay? As the clay is in the potter's hand, so are you in my hand" (Jeremiah 18:3-6).

We are clay; he is the potter. And now we have a choice, of which Paul reminds Timothy:

> In a wealthy home some utensils are made of gold and silver, and some are made of wood and clay. The expensive utensils are used for special occasions, and the cheap ones are for everyday use. If you keep yourself pure, you will be a special utensil for honorable use. Your life will be clean, and you will be ready for the Master to use you for every good work (2 Timothy 2:20-21).

That good work comes through the power of the Spirit within us. "We now have this light shining in our hearts, but we ourselves are like fragile clay jars containing this great treasure. This makes it clear that our great power is from God, not from ourselves" (2 Corinthians 4:7). God is the potter, we his clay. He is the splendid power within. And because of that, he gets all the glory.

> *Father, you are the good potter who is continually fashioning me into a receptacle for your glory. Thank you. I realize that I am clay footed. I know you are the Creator of all good things. I don't always understand the idea that you choose some and not others, or that you display your wrath through some and not others, but I choose right now to trust your ways in my life. Amen.*

Day 52

Read Romans 9:25-29

Concerning Israel, Isaiah the prophet cried out,
"Though the people of Israel are as numerous as the
sand of the seashore, only a remnant will be saved.
For the LORD will carry out his sentence upon
the earth quickly and with finality."

ROMANS 9:27-28

A remnant is the end of a bolt of fabric or the remainder of what was. It's the last part, what holds on, the people who stay for the fifth ovation. God's heart for the nation of Israel was that they would be a shining beacon of hope for the remaining world. They were to display his goodness, wooing the entire human race to himself.

Yet they did not fulfill that high calling. Drenched in idolatry and hampered by sin, they bent themselves toward violence and filth. When they plunged headlong into the very world they were to "save," customs and patterns of behavior that were once vile to them became friends. They lost their prophetic imagination.

Even so, God always had a plan. Though his longing was to see the nation of Israel welcome the Gentiles to himself, he understood the nature of humanity—that a plan based on their fickle obedience would be doomed to fail. So he remedied the situation by sending his Son to be the light the Israelites weren't. That Son experienced the temptations all people faced, yet with rigorous integrity. Because of this, he could call the Gentiles to his fold, calling them children. And he would rescue a remnant of the Jews, the remainder of those left who still longed for his glory and plan.

This plan was dependent solely on God's *hesed*, a rich Hebrew word that simply means loyal, covenantal love. Because God's rescue mission relied on no one but himself (in the three persons of the Trinity), it would succeed. And we are the children of this life-death-resurrection plan, wholly folded into his family because of what Jesus did for us.

And now? We have a ministry to the ends of the world, to be light to those who walk in darkness. The very plan God set into motion with the nation of Israel is mantled upon us. Today, walk in light of that calling. Shine your rescue for all to see.

> *Father, I appreciate your wise plan, how you became what we could not so we could become your children. Thank you for your loyal love, your patience, and your great wisdom. Show me today where I can shine your light for all to see. I want to love like you. I want to live like Jesus did on this earth, full of light. Through your Spirit, empower me today. Amen.*

Day 53

Read Romans 9:30-33

Even though the Gentiles were not trying to follow God's standards, they were made right with God. And it was by faith that this took place. But the people of Israel, who tried so hard to get right with God by keeping the law, never succeeded. Why not? Because they were trying to get right with God by keeping the law instead of by trusting in him.

ROMANS 9:30-32

Trust. Faith. Belief. These are what God is after in our lives. But we so often try to decorate our disobedience, hoping we can mask the fact that we simply don't trust the character or provision of God. This is the overwhelming mistake the first-century Jews made—a pattern the people had lived in for many, many years.

You see this dynamic in Jesus's interactions with the Pharisees, who dotted every *i* and crossed every *t* of the law and yet missed God-in-the-flesh standing in front of them. Rule following will never usher in relationship, but we try so hard to make that round peg fit into the square hole of our own strength.

As we've seen throughout Paul's letter to the Romans, we can never be made right with God through our own volition. We cannot work our way into salvation. No good that we do outweighs the sentence of sin on our hearts. We are helpless, in need of rescue from someone stronger than us. Which is why we all need Jesus.

And Jesus is both God and man, which means he is a person. And since he is a person, we can have a relationship with him. When we see him, we should not walk around him or stumble over him. We are to stop, bow before him, allow for his rescuing reach, and spend our lives in communion with him. This is the essential nature of trust.

I love how Paul reminds us of Old Testament scriptures, Isaiah 28:16 and 8:14. Look at the wording of the former: "This is what the Sovereign LORD says: 'Look! I am placing a foundation stone in Jerusalem, a firm and tested stone. It is a precious cornerstone that is safe to build on. Whoever believes need never be shaken.'" Note that the One saying this is sovereign, reigning supreme. And what he offers is something precious (his Son). We also see that pivotal word, *believe*.

When we exercise belief, we don't step over the rock in our path as if it is an inconvenience or nothing at all. We recognize it as the very foundation of our lives, and we, by trust, build our lives on it accordingly.

> *Father, I don't want to stumble over Jesus. I don't want to treat him as nothing at all. No, I want to follow him, trust him, believe in him. I no longer want to rely on my own strength to impress you, but to surrender everything to the One who surrendered everything for me. This is relationship, not robotic works. This is affection, not detached observance. Amen.*

ROMANS 10

Declarations are important. This is my song of
simply saying I believe in Jesus.

I DECLARE

Earthly wisdom tells me
To perform to curry favor
Preferring my perfection to holy surrender
But God, your way is different
You've already made a way
And I revel in your grace upon grace

CHORUS
Today I declare
That Jesus is Lord
And I wholeheartedly believe
That our resurrecting God
Raised Jesus from the dead
I'm alive
I am saved
I'm set free

My zeal's been misdirected
Trying to work for approval
Trusting my efforts to save my soul
But God, your way is so free
Your work is completed
So I rest in your unchanging love

BRIDGE
Of his love, he gives freely
Oh his life, he laid down
Of his will, he surrendered
To the praise of his renown
Of his grace, oh he lavishes
Oh his heart, how it's pure
Of his gift, he has given
Yes, our God, he endures

Day 54

Read Romans 10:1-4

*They don't understand God's way of making people right
with himself. Refusing to accept God's way, they cling to
their own way of getting right with God by trying to keep
the law. For Christ has already accomplished the purpose
for which the law was given. As a result, all who believe
in him are made right with God.*

ROMANS 10:3-4

These five words should shake us all down to the core of ourselves:
"refusing to accept God's way." When we think we're cleverer,
stronger, or better than the Almighty God, we join the Jewish people
who missed the significance of the Messiah standing before them. They
spent so much time try-try-trying to get right in their own strength,
that they failed to realize they never could. They stopped believing they
needed a Messiah. Instead, they spent their lives becoming their own
little messiahs, yet with futility and frustration.

We can do the same thing. When we live a life devoid of Christ yet
full of Christian activities, we miss Jesus. When we study the Word of
God without obeying it through the power of the Holy Spirit, preferring our own rules to the gentle rule of the Spirit, we miss Jesus. When
we misdirect our zeal toward causes or a personal holiness campaign in
our own strength, we miss Jesus.

When we try to live the Christian life apart from the Spirit of God
indwelling us, we essentially say we are clinging to our own way of

getting right with God. Which is simply worshipping ourselves rather than surrendering to the Almighty God. If something depends on us, we rely on our strength. But if everything we need for a life of obedience depends on Jesus, we rely on the Spirit.

Truth: Christ has already accomplished our right standing with God. He finished the work. We currently are right before God. There's nothing we can do to add to our rightness. What God requires is belief and trust. He asks us to receive the gift of right standing, realizing we were helpless and could not save ourselves. Then our lives will overflow with gratitude, and we will naturally rely on the power of the Holy Spirit within us to accomplish the work he wants us to do.

It's never been about you making a showing to God. It's always about him showing his faithfulness to you.

> *Father, thank you for revealing yourself through Jesus Christ. Help me live in belief. I realize that you have sent the Spirit to live within me, giving me the ability to surrender again to you. I can't live this life of faith on my own. I am helpless. But because you have rescued me and sent me the Helper, I can approach today with joyful confidence. Amen.*

Day 55

Read Romans 10:5-13

If you openly declare that Jesus is Lord and believe in your heart
that God raised him from the dead, you will be saved. For it
is by believing in your heart that you are made right with God,
and it is by openly declaring your faith that you are saved.

ROMANS 10:9-10

Paul is laying out a careful argument here about the veracity of Christ and his pivotal role in our salvation. He references Old Testament verses, providing an exegesis of scriptures to hone his point. Those verses are (in order): Leviticus 18:5; Deuteronomy 30:12-14; Isaiah 28:16; and Joel 2:32. I find it fascinating that these are also listed chronologically as you find them in the Law and the Prophets, which shows Paul's careful survey of the Old Testament.

These scriptures bookend the central truth of the gospel. If someone were to ask you how to be made right with God, you could respond with these verses about declaration and belief. We declare that which we believe about Jesus Christ—that he died, yes, but that his resurrection is historical fact, and because of the resurrection, he is Lord of everything.

Because of what was previously written, we see that Jesus did everything necessary to secure our salvation—coming from heaven, making his home on earth with humanity while perfectly fulfilling every mandate of the law, then descending into death and coming out of death's doorway utterly victorious.

Jesus did not merely do this for his "own" people, the Jews. He came to set the entire world free—a gift for humanity, completing the story of salvation for everyone who dares to believe.

Perhaps you have demonstrated this belief in the gospel, but have you declared it? In the beginning of Romans, Paul talks about not being ashamed of the gospel. To declare your faith out loud is to show the world you are not ashamed of the scandal of grace. Although we proclaim this quite openly at baptism, we have opportunities every day to declare that which we already know to be true. Perhaps today is one of those days.

> *Father, how can I thank you for sending your Son to live, die, and rise on my behalf? I do believe! And I also want to proclaim that belief. I acknowledge that Jesus is Lord, and I choose today to live out that belief. Bring opportunities my way today to share my belief with others—not in an obnoxious way, but in a manner that brings them to you. Amen.*

Day 56

Read Romans 10:14-17

How can they call on him to save them unless they believe in him? And how can they believe in him if they have never heard about him? And how can they hear about him unless someone tells them? And how will anyone go and tell them without being sent? That is why the Scriptures say, "How beautiful are the feet of messengers who bring good news!"

ROMANS 10:14-15

Again we see Paul returning to the Old Testament to make his argument that the gospel is for all humankind. Throughout the Bible we see God pursue his people, the nation of Israel. How crazy it must've been for Jesus when the upholders of the Jewish law (which he both created and fulfilled completely) missed him. Here he was, God in the flesh, standing and breathing before them, yet the leaders forfeited worshipping him and instead sought to silence and kill him. Why? Because of envy. "[Pilate] realized by now that the leading priests had arrested Jesus out of envy" (Mark 15:10).

Why envy? Perhaps that had something to do with control. The Jewish leaders had the corner on the market of salvation. They controlled the narrative of who was in and who was out. And since they had that control, they could consolidate power. Yet when Jesus entered their circle, he kept messing with their message. His theology was a welcoming party, not an exclusive club for the elite. And because he welcomed all (as was always God's intention), the masses followed him everywhere. His popularity soared.

With that kind of "fame," the Pharisees could no longer control the masses and keep them under their narrow theological thumbs. Their way of interacting with people caused a dwindling of following (as legalism is apt to do), but Jesus's way of love and radical inclusion, even to—gasp!—Gentiles and Samaritans, irresistibly drew others. Envy invaded the hearts of the Jewish leaders, and that envy led to crucifixion.

You can hear echoes of God's longing for all people to be saved through Paul's pleading. In order for people to hear, others have to share. We who are now personal witnesses to this all-welcoming salvation have the joyful privilege of bringing this Good News to the world. In Ephesians, Paul writes about our feet being shod with the gospel of peace (6:15 NASB), and with these feet, we bring the Good News to as many as we can.

> *Father, thank you for sending your Son to all people, to radically save anyone who calls upon his name. I pray today my response would be both worship and walking. I want to praise you moment by moment for rescuing me, but I also want to walk into places where you are not yet named and share my story (your story!) of being set free. Amen.*

Day 57

Read Romans 10:18-21

Did the people of Israel really understand? Yes, they did, for even in the time of Moses, God said, "I will rouse your jealousy through people who are not even a nation. I will provoke your anger through the foolish Gentiles."

ROMANS 10:19

I find it fascinating that God predicted the Jewish leaders' envy years and years before Jesus arrived on earth. He came to set all people free, even the "foolish Gentiles," which was always a part of his plan. His desire, shown throughout the Old Testament, was that all people would come to know him, which is why Israel was to be a beacon of salvation. Consider this proclamation from God in Isaiah: "You will do more than restore the people of Israel to me. I will make you a light to the Gentiles, and you will bring my salvation to the ends of the earth" (49:6).

In this passage, Paul quotes Psalm 19:4, Deuteronomy 32:21 and Isaiah 65:1-2 to further illustrate God's desire for the entire world. Yes, God's people, the nation of Israel, held a special place in his heart—after all, Jesus is of Jewish descent. It was God's ever-enlarging plan to move from one chosen nation to an entire world of chosen people, but Israel hoarded its privilege.

Throughout the Old Testament we see this God of pursuit wooing, preparing, helping, giving instruction, providing a king (though he was their rightful King), rebuking, exiling, disciplining, and providing a remnant. God welcomed his people with open arms, but their constant response was rebellion and running away. Disobedience ruled their hearts.

And the truth is, all of us are in this state when we're living under the penalty and scrutiny of sin. We can't help but let disobedience push us away from the God who saves. This is not merely a rebuke for the Jews, but an indication of a humanity problem—this desire to live life on our own terms apart from the One who created us.

God is the pursuer of our hearts. He holds out his hand of reconciliation to all people. He first extended this to the nation of Israel, then reached through them to touch the rest of the world. We all have a choice: to grasp that hand of rescue or run a hundred miles the other way. Which will you choose?

Father, thank you for being a God of pursuit. I hear the agony of your cries as you reach out to the Jews and the people reaching the ends of the earth. It is your desire that we would all be reconciled to yourself. Thank you for making a way. I choose today to run into your welcoming embrace. Amen.

ROMANS 11

Our God is then. He is now. He is in the future.
All that astounds me, makes me want to worship.

WAS, IS, WILL BE

You were there
In my past
Where regret stranded my joy

You are there
In today
When fear strangles my voice

You'll be there
In tomorrow
Completing your started work

CHORUS
God of then
God of now
God of next
How I worship you
You were there
You are here
You will reign
How I worship you

BRIDGE
My past cannot negate your glory
My present can't nullify your story
My future—alive and soaring
All because of you

Day 58

Read Romans 11:1-4

Elijah the prophet complained to God about the people of Israel and said, "LORD, they have killed your prophets and torn down your altars. I am the only one left, and now they are trying to kill me, too." And do you remember God's reply? He said, "No, I have 7,000 others who have never bowed down to Baal!"

ROMANS 11:2-4

To understand Elijah's despair, we must know what he faced in his culture. Worship of the Canaanite god Baal was rampant—it permeated the practices and beliefs of the surrounding culture, and it had, sadly, invaded the Israelite religion. Baal was known as the god who provided rain and provision for crops—he was the Canaanites' powerful agricultural god. He was, to them, the giver of life. To appease this angry-looking deity, all sorts of terrible things had to be done involving sexual deviance and death—as worship involved temple prostitution and child sacrifice.

But Elijah knew only God would be worshipped, which we see in his interaction with the prophets of Baal in 1 Kings 18, when God showed himself infinitely more powerful than this earthly god. When Elijah neared his own breaking point as a prophet, feeling alone in his worship of the Almighty God, God reminded him that he was not. A remnant remained.

This idea of a remnant is a powerful one. It shows that when God chooses a people, he does not abandon them. He empowers those who faithfully remain to stay true to him and his kingdom. We see this in the Noahic covenant (Genesis 9:8-17), where God eradicates the land of violence, but spares a remnant (Noah's family) and vows never to flood the whole earth again. We see this concept of a remnant again after the exile to Babylon, when Nehemiah returns and rebuilds the toppled-over walls of Jerusalem. And we see this powerfully when Jesus comes to earth to rescue humanity from themselves.

We, now, are that remnant. We choose, by the power of the Holy Spirit, to bow down only to the King of kings, the Lord of lords. We are the offspring of God's long-awaited plan, enacted through the nation of Israel, traced through the lineage of Christ. We have been saved from certain death so we may worship the God of life. Let's thank him for that.

> *Father, thank you that you didn't ultimately reject Israel, but you always reserved a remnant, and from that remnant came the life of Jesus Christ. I'm utterly humbled to be a part of that remnant today. Help me live in gratitude in light of that truth. Thank you for choosing me. Thank you for grafting me into your family. Amen.*

Day 59

Read Romans 11:5-10

A few of the people of Israel have remained faithful because of God's grace—his undeserved kindness in choosing them. And since it is through God's kindness, then it is not by their good works. For in that case, God's grace would not be what it really is—free and undeserved.

ROMANS 11:5-6

We see the kindness of God highlighted throughout Romans. It's not his harsh severity that beckons us to himself—it's his merciful kindness. Paul calls it "undeserved," for that is the truth. We have done nothing to deserve this surprising favor. And though the nation of Israel often tried to make themselves right through observation of the law, none of that merited God's choosing. His choice of them was pure, unadulterated grace.

We have to remember that the kingdom of God is not a democracy, but a kingdom—ruled by a powerful, yet benevolent King. Because he rules this world, he has sovereignty over his kingdom. While that may be intimidating or seem unfair in light of our democratic leanings, God's volition is actually spectacularly confounding. He is perfection. He is love. He is all-seeing, all-knowing, all-powerful. And yet? He chooses us. He condescended to come to earth, sending his Son to die for us. It's a beautiful conundrum that God, who is all-sufficient in himself, would so love his creation that way.

Yes, some of Israel remains blind to this undeserved kindness. They are in a deep sleep until the next phase of God's plan gloriously unfolds. In the meantime, we pray. We trust the hand and heart of God. We rejoice in the uncanny way that he has called us friends. We spend our lives for the One who spent his life for us. And we keep our hearts unstained from the world. Why? Because we choose to see those who don't yet know him as a cautionary tale. We understand what a privilege it is to be called children of God. We know how easily we can slip into the blindness or stubbornness of unbelief. Today? We rest in the favor of God and the powerful kindness he uses to draw us to himself.

Father, I pray for those who don't yet know you, particularly my Jewish brothers and sisters who cannot yet see who Jesus is. Bring them back to yourself. In the meantime, I remain utterly grateful for all you've done. I cannot believe you have chosen me to be your child and bear fruit. I love you for that. Keep me from blindness and stubbornness today. Amen.

Day 60

Read Romans 11:11-16

Did God's people stumble and fall beyond recovery?
Of course not! They were disobedient, so God made salvation
available to the Gentiles. But he wanted his own people to
become jealous and claim it for themselves. Now if the Gentiles
were enriched because the people of Israel turned down God's
offer of salvation, think how much greater a blessing
the world will share when they finally accept it.

ROMANS 11:11-12

God's plan has always involved the entirety of the human race. Beginning with one man and one woman who chose a pathway away from him, moving through the patriarch Abraham and his offspring, through kings and kingdoms, judges and prophets, faithfulness and rightful exile, to the glorious dawning of Jesus come to earth, God has been wooing humanity to himself.

His heart? To see all people bow before him, not in indentured servitude, but in glorious relationship full of gratitude. His calling of the nation of Israel is irrevocable; his favor upon them is resolute. It was through them that Jesus came to earth, and they will play a key role as the world comes to an end.

In the meantime, those who know Christ, yet are without Jewish descent, experience the privilege it is to know God and be known by him. We are now his children. While the Old Testament highlighted the temple of God, *we* are now his temple, inhabited by the Holy Spirit.

We bear the image of our Savior and, together with our brothers and sisters around the world, comprise the body of Christ.

We are living in the age of grace. We have been made holy by the life, death, and resurrection of Jesus. We live in the privilege of son- and daughter-ship. We are loved by God, and never, ever left alone or forsaken. This promise of his presence, like the cloud during the day and the pillar of fire at night for the wandering Israelites, is always available. What a privilege it is to be called his children—well loved, sought, and died for. His holiness has made us whole, and he has set us apart to be light to a darkened world.

Father, being chosen by you is something I need to internalize. When life is hard and takes strange turns, I can rest on the unchanging fact of your choosing. You have remade me. You have given me new life. You have loved me far more than I deserve. Thank you. When my emotions careen, help me settle myself on the bedrock of this truth: You have chosen me. Amen.

Day 61

Read Romans 11:17-21

Some of these branches from Abraham's tree—some of the people of Israel—have been broken off. And you Gentiles, who were branches from a wild olive tree, have been grafted in. So now you also receive the blessing God has promised Abraham and his children, sharing in the rich nourishment from the root of God's special olive tree. But you must not brag about being grafted in to replace the branches that were broken off. You are just a branch, not the root.

ROMANS 11:17-18

It is common practice these days for grapevine rootstocks to differ from their vines because the vines are grafted into a different species. In the 1800s, the European wine-making industry experienced near extermination because of the proliferation of *phylloxera*, an invasive vine pest. Thankfully, a Texan horticulturist named T.V. Munson discovered resistant rootstocks in Texas. Once vintners replaced their susceptible roots with the Texas rootstock, the vineyards came back to life.[17]

This clearly demonstrates the symbiosis of the roots and the vines. We cannot have one without the other. And the roots must be strong to resist an onslaught of pests. In this illustration, Paul reminds Gentiles that they are grafted into the rootstock of the nation of Israel—a perfect marriage of necessity and reliance. Without the roots, the vines would wither, but without the vines, the roots would produce no fruit.

Those who have Jewish heritage can rightly revel in the covenants God made with them. God's glory resides there within the rootstock. And those who have been carefully grafted in by the Gardener of us all can rightly revel in the privilege of continuing the story of the New Covenant. What a powerful heritage we have! Without the strong roots, we could not bear fruit. This is nothing to be a braggart about; instead, we should humbly thank Jesus for what it cost him as the Vinedresser— his blood shed for us.

Once we were severed limbs, trying in vain to reconcile with a holy God. But now he has gloriously connected us to himself. It is sheer gift, and our response should be worship and gratitude. We can read John 15 with new eyes, no longer resisting pruning, but welcoming it—all for the sake of our growth and potential fruit.

Father, I've been grafted in! Thank you for that. Thank you for the heritage rootstock you've prepared and connected me to. My relationship with you is not finite, but spans eons— through Jesus, the exile, the nation of Israel, Noah's family, and Adam and Eve. Keep me connected to the root. Prune me so I can bear more fruit for you. Amen.

Day 62

Read Romans 11:22-24

Notice how God is both kind and severe. He is severe toward those who disobeyed, but kind to you if you continue to trust in his kindness. But if you stop trusting, you also will be cut off. And if the people of Israel turn from their unbelief, they will be grafted in again, for God has the power to graft them back into the tree.

ROMANS 11:22-23

You might read this passage and worry. *Will I be cut off? Can I lose my salvation?* While we tend to highlight verses about the kindness of God, our highlighter stops speeding across the page when God's severity is mentioned—most likely because it confuses us.

This is why it's desperately important to read the whole counsel of Scripture when you're forming and reforming your theology. Remember, what you think about God changes everything about your life. It matters. And how you think about him affects the way you live your life. If you pick and choose scriptures to suit your pet theology, you may find yourself stressed when you read a passage like today's.

In times like this, remind yourself of what you know about God's character. Yes, he is kind. But yes, he is also severe. Yes, he is love. But yes, he is also just. In fact, justice is woven into his character, which is something we should rejoice about, not shy away from. God's perfect justice means that those who continually act evil without repentance will pay for their crimes against humanity. It means that the cries of victims around the world are heard. They may suffer on this earth (and oh, how we grieve about that), but ultimately, God will right the wrongs and judge everyone fairly.

We are not saved by our own works of righteousness. Those attempts, Scripture says, are like "filthy rags" (Isaiah 64:6). God is the initiator of our salvation. He pursued us and sent his Son to die for us so we could be made right. That is an assured fact. These verses in Romans are leveled at those who have heard about God's kindness and severity, but have chosen willfully to neglect such a great salvation. They have turned away from this beautiful gift. There are certainly repercussions for doing so, but that judgment does not mean your salvation is fickle, dependent on your perfection. No, your salvation is a gift from the perfect One.

> *Father, thank you for your righteousness. Thank you that you will one day judge this world, and thank you that I don't have to! I am utterly grateful for your gift of salvation, for making me right when all I could do was wrong. Thank you for the finality of "It is finished." Thank you that I can live with assurance of my standing before you because it doesn't depend on my faithfulness, but yours. Amen.*

Day 63

Read Romans 11:25-27

I want you to understand this mystery, dear brothers and sisters, so that you will not feel proud about yourselves. Some of the people of Israel have hard hearts, but this will last only until the full number of Gentiles comes to Christ.

ROMANS 11:25

Not everything in the Christian life is easily understood. Christianity is not merely a set of doctrines etched in stone with no nuance of interpretations—it's a relationship with a dynamic, powerful Creator. That's why Paul calls this relationship between God and Israel a mystery. It's not quickly figured out. The word Paul uses for *mystery* in today's verse is *musterion,* which means something hidden. "In the Bible, a 'mystery'...is *not something unknowable.* Rather, it is what *can only be known through revelation,* i.e. because *God reveals* it."[18] We cannot untangle the entire story here. But we can rely on the character of God.

How can we read today's scripture with eyes of faith? It helps to discern the main point of the passage: Israel is hard hearted, but someday that will change. If we place ourselves in that narrative, we are reminded of our own similar pathway. There was a time when our hearts were hardened toward the things of God, when we had no desire to love or follow our Creator. Embittered by sin and in love with the flashiness of the world, we thought we had no need of God.

But eventually, the wooing of the Spirit brought us face-to-face with the reality of our condition. We were utterly helpless, mired in sin, with no ability to save ourselves. This is when Christ intervened. His life, death, and resurrection created a narrow pathway of invitation to us. Where we once were outsiders, we are now inside, enjoying the fellowship of God.

This will be Israel's journey as well. Currently, many representing Israel are far from Jesus. But God's mysterious plan (yet to be revealed) will unfold, and in that powerful moment, those who once had hardened hearts will clearly see who Jesus is. He will usher them onto the narrow pathway because he is the way. He promises he will take away their sins, just as he did for us.

This now-and-not-yet redemption should cause us to celebrate. No, we won't always understand every mystery (if we did, we'd be God), but we can trust the One who holds the mystery because he has proven himself worthy of our trust.

Father, thank you for pursuing me when my heart was hardened against you. I swam in my disobedience, loved my fellowship with the world. But eventually I saw through all the shiny things the world had to offer, and I met you in the midst of my despair. Thank you for pursuing me, rescuing me, and setting me free. I pray for my Jewish brothers and sisters, that you would continue to beckon them near. Amen.

Day 64

Read Romans 11:28-36

Oh, how great are God's riches and wisdom and knowledge! How impossible it is for us to understand his decisions and his ways! For who can know the LORD's thoughts? Who knows enough to give him advice? And who has given him so much that he needs to pay it back? For everything comes from him and exists by his power and is intended for his glory. All glory to him forever! Amen.

ROMANS 11:33-36

Throughout Scripture, we hear echoes of the last part of Romans 11, where we taste the magnificence and power of God. When people encounter just a hint of him, they cannot help but fall facedown in awe, fear, and reverence. And when Jesus confounded people with his innate wisdom while on earth, he stunned his listeners. Simply put, God is entirely *other* than us. He exists within himself as sufficient, all-knowing, holding every secret. His plan is inscrutable, and his ways are often mysterious.

The prophet Isaiah echoes Paul: "'My thoughts are nothing like your thoughts,' says the LORD. 'And my ways are far beyond anything you could imagine. For just as the heavens are higher than the earth, so my ways are higher than your ways and my thoughts higher than your thoughts'" (Isaiah 55:8-9). Paul returns to this idea of God's otherness in his letter to the Ephesians: "All glory to God, who is able, through his mighty power at work within us, to accomplish infinitely more than we might ask or think. Glory to him in the church and in Christ Jesus through all generations forever and ever! Amen" (3:20-21).

When problems loom large, and our fear dwarfs our faith, we must remind ourselves of this central truth. God is bigger than our pain, worries, fears, and very real circumstances. His ways are higher. While the tension will always exist when we face trials—it is human to wonder where God is in the midst of pain—training our minds to remember the greatness of God will give us much-needed perspective. He holds the world in the cup of his hands. He has a plan for redemption—a plan he is painstakingly working on behind the veil of heaven. He will vanquish evil once and for all. One day, we will exhale all the pain of our earthly lives as we marvel at the intricate way God has woven all stories for his glory.

Father, you are higher than my highest thought, smarter than my wisest calculation. You are greater than my looming fear. You are holy, holy, holy. You are beautifully strong. Your plan is immovable. Help me in the midst of my trial to remind myself of your ability, not my inability. I feel small, but I rest in your vastness. Amen.

ROMANS 12

My favorite chapter of Romans calls for surrender,
working alongside others, and loving others well.

WHOLLY TO YOU

How I treat others
Is how I treat you
So empower my heart to love well
You don't prefer favorites
Dignifying the broken
Your affection poured out on us all

CHORUS

I give myself
Wholly to you
A sacrifice of praise
I lay me down
Please transform me
By your outrageous grace

All of us gifted
By your sovereign hand
Please free up our lives to serve well
Your body, it's varied
And pride must be buried
All using our gifts for your smile

BRIDGE

We belong to you
We belong to each other
We surrender our lives to your plan
We belong to you
We belong to each other
We courageously trust in your hand

Day 65

Read Romans 12:1-2

*And so, dear brothers and sisters, I plead with you to give your
bodies to God because of all he has done for you. Let them be a
living and holy sacrifice—the kind he will find acceptable.
This is truly the way to worship him.*

ROMANS 12:1

There's a tendency to rob these popular verses of their context. It makes sense. This section of Scripture has layers of wisdom as well as practical application for the believer. But we must look back to yesterday's passage, which reminds us that God is infinitely greater than us. He is powerfully intelligent. His ways are not always easy to discern. He is God. We are not.

The "and so" at the beginning of today's verse piggybacks on this notion. Because of God's sometimes-unsearchable landscape, we have some choices to make about how we live our lives. In light of his mysterious plan, Paul shows us how we are to conduct ourselves in this sin-infected world.

First, he hearkens us back to the Old Testament sacrificial system, reminding us that we are now the offering. Our bodies are the sacrifice. Once the Holy Spirit only alighted upon some, but we now live in an age of his continual presence. How much more, then, should we live in gratitude? And that gratitude for God-with-us echoes what Jesus did for us. Jesus sacrificed for us. Jesus gave his body for us. He laid down his life. To worship God, then, is not to sing songs on a Sunday morning. No, to worship is simply to obey him. Laying down your life, saying prayers like, "Father, you are stronger and smarter than me. You have done so much. I willingly lay down my resolve, my will, and my entire body in worship. Tell me what to do, and I will obey you." Obedience, as it's said often in Scripture, is "better than sacrifice" (for example, see 1 Samuel 15:22).

Once you've obeyed God by offering up your body, there's another area of life that needs reformation—your mind. Paul knows that how we live (in obedience or disobedience) flows from our beliefs about God. The problem is, we are constantly attacked by a world that tries to get us to think wrongly about God, our state, the nature of sin, and what is truly valuable. The only way to transform our thinking is to ask God to sift through the cacophony of lies and false messages so we'll know the truth. This truth will set us free (see John 8:32). It will enable us to see clearly the will of God. The messages of the world are meant to deceive, sideline, and sidetrack us from the narrow road (*Accumulate wealth! Look a certain way! Sacrifice your soul for success! Be your own made-in-your-image god!*), but the message of redemption is meant to keep us close to our Creator.

> *Father, help me focus wholeheartedly on who you are and revel in your magnificence and power. In light of your nature, I choose today to offer myself afresh, to give you my body and mind. I know I've coddled lies to myself. I know I've looked far too longingly on what this world calls success. Rein me in. Keep me close to you. Speak truth over me so I'll abandon the lies. Amen.*

Day 66

Read Romans 12:3-5

Because of the privilege and authority God has given me, I give each of you this warning: Don't think you are better than you really are. Be honest in your evaluation of yourselves, measuring yourselves by the faith God has given us.

ROMANS 12:3

When Paul warns us, we should pay attention. He shares his heart because of his great love for the body of Christ. All believers around the world make up this body, which is varied, unique, and essential. Unfortunately, in today's climate, we create little hierarchies of privilege within the church. Those with up-front gifts receive accolades and applause. Those who serve quietly are forgotten, relegated to back rooms. And yet, when Jesus walked the earth, he practically ran to the forgotten, and he reserved his harshest criticism for those preening in the limelight.

Remember Jesus's words to the disciples who were trying to curry favor, jockeying for heavenly position:

> You know that the rulers in this world lord it over their people, and officials flaunt their authority over those under them. But among you it will be different. Whoever wants to be a leader among you must be your servant, and whoever wants to be first among you must become your slave. For even the Son of Man came not to be served but to serve

others and to give his life as a ransom for many (Matthew 20:25-28).

The body of Christ works best when we have this humble-servant mind-set. When we long to serve others, we obey these verses in Romans. We consider others as more important than ourselves, no matter their gifting. We stop judging others because we spend our time serving. We subjugate our will beneath the better good of others. We assess ourselves with dogged self-awareness, alert to our own flaws, yet generous toward others as they battle theirs.

Good communicators understand this dynamic. They highlight their foibles and herald other people's triumphs. In doing so, they endear themselves to audiences. We have an audience of One, who sent his Son to die for every single human being, plays no favorites, and loves us all. To worship him is to be kind and gracious to the ones he loves. And when the church works together like this in harmony, the world takes notice.

Father, help me be self-aware. Grant me insight to judge myself fairly, yet offer generosity to others. Forgive me for sometimes thinking people with flashy gifts are more important. Show me someone working diligently behind the scenes of your church this week so I can specifically serve and encourage them. I want to be like Jesus, humbly serving. Amen.

Day 67

Read Romans 12:6-8

In his grace, God has given us different gifts for doing certain things well. So if God has given you the ability to prophesy, speak out with as much faith as God has given you. If your gift is serving others, serve them well. If you are a teacher, teach well.

ROMANS 12:6-7

In this exhortation part of Romans, Paul uses an if/then structure. If God has given you *this*, then do *this*. God's gifts are intended to be used, not neglected or squandered.

We see this clearly in Jesus's teaching of the talents. The story begins with a nobleman who entrusts varying levels of money to his servants, goes away, then returns. This is what he discovered: "The servant who received the five bags of silver began to invest the money and earned five more. The servant with two bags of silver also went to work and earned two more. But the servant who received the one bag of silver dug a hole in the ground and hid the master's money" (Matthew 25:16-18).

Regarding the final servant who buried the money, the nobleman declares, "Take the money from this servant, and give it to the one with the ten bags of silver. To those who use well what they are given, even more will be given, and they will have an abundance. But from those who do nothing, even what little they have will be taken away" (verses 28-29).

This story is sandwiched between the story of the ten bridesmaids (some were ready for the wedding; some were not) and Jesus's words about the final judgment. With this parable strategically placed between the two, we clearly see that what we do on this earth has eternal significance. When God gifts us, our proper response is to use those gifts with gusto in service to the kingdom—in light of eternity.

The words Paul uses in Romans after noting each gift are fascinating. Those who prophesy do so with *pisteos* (faith). With speakers, servants, and encouragers, Paul uses nearly the same words—in other words, in your serving, serve; in your teaching, teach; in your encouraging, encourage. He finishes by speaking of giving with generosity (*haploteti*). Those who lead are to do so with zeal (*spoude*), and those who show kindness are to do so with hilarity (*hilaroteti*). So not only are we to use the gifts God has given us, but we are to respond with zealous hilarity and faithful generosity. This is Paul's explanation of the surrender he taught in verses 1-2, the presentation of our bodies as offerings. We worship by vigorously exercising our gifts—not grudgingly, but joyfully.

> *Father, help me remember that it's a privilege to serve you. I'm so grateful you've given gifts to your followers. Help me discern mine. Show me through Scripture, the encouragement of others, and my own intuition. I do want to serve you with everything I have. And if you give me five talents, I pray I would multiply them and not bury them in fear. I need zealous hilarity and faithful generosity when it comes to responding to your gifts. Amen.*

Day 68

Read Romans 12:9-13

Don't just pretend to love others. Really love them. Hate what is wrong. Hold tightly to what is good. Love each other with genuine affection, and take delight in honoring each other.

ROMANS 12:9-10

The word *pretend* has rich meaning. The phrase "Don't just pretend" in the New Living Translation is *anypokritos* in the Greek, and it means the opposite of hypocrisy. We see the word appear in James as well: "The wisdom from above is first of all pure. It is also peace loving, gentle at all times, and willing to yield to others. It is full of mercy and the fruit of good deeds. It shows no favoritism and is always *sincere*" (3:17, emphasis mine). We are to have authentic, genuine love for others, not feigning our love, and certainly not preferring certain people because of their status.

Love notices the outcast and deems him or her worthy of affection. In fact, Paul encourages us to love others (he didn't state which "type" of others) "with genuine affection" (12:10). Part of that affection lies in the word *proegeomai* (translated as "honoring" in the New Living Translation), which is only used once in the New Testament. This word literally means going before. (This echoes Jesus's teaching in Matthew 20:16, where he reminds us that kingdom math is entirely different than the world's calculations: "Those who are last now will be first then, and those who are first will be last.")

Take note that all these commands Paul levels our way have to do with community. When we love, community flourishes. When we hate what is evil and grasp goodness, justice prevails in the lives of those we serve. When we give others the first place in line, an ethos of kindness reigns. When we take seriously God's encouragement to work hard, our entire community (friends, family, neighbors) flourishes. When we exhibit hope, we inspire others to do the same. When we endure trials, we empower others to face theirs with grit. When we pray, God answers—deepening our faith, blessing our relationship with him—and the subject of our prayers is often other people. When we help others in need, we show the world that generosity, not stinginess, is our way of life. And practicing hospitality welcomes all people, reveals the feast of God, and reminds us that we are all image bearers of God.

There is always a so-what to the story God is writing in your life. You are blessed to be a blessing. Loved to love others. Endowed to pass on the wealth—whether material or spiritual. Helped to be a helper. Encouraged so that you can encourage others (see 1 Corinthians 1:4-7). All this is done with authenticity and openheartedness—to the praise of the One who gave it all to us in the first place. He graces. We grace.

> *Father, thank you for this reminder today. I want to be a generous believer who loves others without preference. Help me reorient my mind-set from focusing on myself and my needs to focusing on the needs of the community. You have given me so much, and I want to mimic your kindness on the pavement of my real life. I love you. I need you. I adore you. I worship you. May my gratitude for your goodness flow into the ones I love. Amen.*

Day 69

Read Romans 12:14-21

Bless those who persecute you. Don't curse them; pray that God will bless them. Be happy with those who are happy, and weep with those who weep. Live in harmony with each other. Don't be too proud to enjoy the company of ordinary people. And don't think you know it all!

Romans 12:14-16

What Paul asks of us here is simple: Do as Jesus did. He didn't curse those who persecuted him—instead, he remained silent while accusations flew. He uttered forgiveness from the very instrument of his torture and death (the cross). He rejoiced at the laughter of others (I can picture him reclining around tables with the disciples, enjoying meals and lively conversation). He certainly wept at the tomb of his friend Lazarus. He entered into our world—which means he willingly chose to grieve with humanity.

He lived in harmony with those he fashioned (an astounding thought, the Creator hanging out with the created). He made himself nothing, taking on the form of a bond servant (see Philippians 2:7). And he associated with, dwelled with, walked with people of lower caste. He crossed man-made boundaries, infuriating the religious leaders who didn't dare defile themselves with ordinary folks.

He could have paid us all back with evil for the evil we did, but instead he bore our evil upon his body, bleeding his sacrifice for our salvation. He lived the most honorable life in human history, not seeking his honor, but the Father's. He, the Prince of Peace, pursued peace on earth, and then graced it freely to us in the person of the Holy Spirit after his resurrection.

Though our sin nature earned us vengeance, Jesus, the perfect One, did not enact perfect justice. Instead, he entrusted his own death to the One who had the plan all along—a rescue mission for humanity. Jesus fed his enemies (surely there were a few in the crowd of 5,000). Jesus became living water to those who thirsted (see John 4). He took on shame, and as he did, he vanquished evil by doing the ultimate good— dying on a cross.

He only asks of us what he has already done. And now his strength and power reside in us through the Holy Spirit. It may seem impossible to live a life of sacrificial love, but with the Spirit, all things are possible.

Father, thank you for sending your Son, Jesus, to die in my place. Thank you that he asks me to do only what he has done. He has gone gloriously before me. I need your Spirit to infuse me with the kind of strength that empowers me to love my enemies, pray for them, empathize with others, and trust you for judgment. Oh, how I need your perspective today. Amen.

ROMANS 13

I'm struck by two things in this chapter: the necessity to love and the urgency of life. Both inform this worship song.

THE LOVE DEBT

Time slips from me
The kingdom moves on
The day, it will morph into night
Rushing past hushed dawn
So lead me to love
As time marches on
I don't want to quiet
Your redemptive song

CHORUS
Love doesn't harm
It always rushes in
Love comes from you
Covering our sin
I choose to love
It's what my heart owes

I choose to live
Through life's highs and its lows
Love is the oxygen
We breathe in today
While hate chokes the life
Out of every connection
So lead me to love
A child of resurrection

BRIDGE
I will clothe myself
With your love, oh Lord
I will choose to sing
Your redemption song
Through your strength, I rise
To my feet and run
For your presence, Lord
It informs my joy

Day 70

Read Romans 13:1-5

Everyone must submit to governing authorities.
For all authority comes from God, and those in positions
of authority have been placed there by God.

ROMANS 13:1

Paul uses the plural word for authorities (*exousiais*) here once, then two other times in the New Testament. In Titus 3:1, he parallels his thoughts in Romans 13, referring to governing authorities: "Remind the believers to submit to the government and its officers. They should be obedient, always ready to do what is good." In Ephesians 3:10, he expands the meaning to include the authorities governing the spiritual realms: "God's purpose in all this was to use the church to display his wisdom in its rich variety to all the unseen rulers and authorities in the heavenly places."

Our obedience to God is echoed in our obedience to the laws of our land. Does this mean we should violate God's laws because our laws demand we do so? No. This is why we must take the whole counsel of Scripture into consideration when we're examining a lone passage. Remember the Hebrew midwives who disobeyed Pharaoh's edict that they kill the firstborn boys? They disobeyed because they feared God more than they feared the government (see Exodus 1:15-21). Remember Rahab, who protected the spies? Obadiah, a prophet, willfully hid other prophets from Jezebel, who rampaged on a killing spree (see

1 Kings 18:3-4). In Acts 4, we see Peter telling the authorities that he can't help but teach about Jesus, though they explicitly commanded him not to. So, yes, there are times when civil disobedience is right.

But the thrust of these verses is order. The world operates better when people obey the fair-minded laws of their government. Even Jesus paid taxes (see Matthew 17:24-27). And he subjected himself to the government. He could've extricated himself from the cross, a legion of angels by his side, enacting justice against the Roman government. But he did not. He gave us an example of holy submission. He showed us the power of submitting to others, of patience and living rightly. We do this, too, to exemplify him to others.

Remember that throughout Romans, Paul has an evangelist's heart. Our citizenship is in heaven, but that privilege should inform our earthly decisions. We should live upstanding lives in order to usher in the transfer of non-believers into heavenly citizenship.

Father, I choose today to submit to the laws of my land. I do this because it is right. If there is ever a time I am to disobey the civil authorities, would you show me clearly? I pray for my friends and neighbors who don't yet know you. I pray my good citizenship and kindness are avenues for them to see you. Bring them to yourself today. Amen.

Day 71

Read Romans 13:6-10

Owe nothing to anyone—except for your obligation to love one another. If you love your neighbor, you will fulfill the requirements of God's law.

ROMANS 13:8

Paul begins this passage with money, yet ends with love. The two have been battling each other for millennia. Money, in its rightful place, is a tool. It helps governments and entities do their necessary jobs. In the case of taxes, it paves roads, builds bridges, funds schools, and (hopefully) ensures safety and justice for the citizenry. We demonstrate our respect for those in authority by rendering unto Caesar what is Caesar's (Mark 12:17).

Paul shifts from owing money to owing love. Love, then, becomes a joyful reciprocation, a holy owing. He calls love an "obligation." But when we hear the ring of that word in our ears, we think "robotic" or "rote." On the contrary, love is the choice we make daily.

Because Jesus demonstrated sacrificial love toward us, our response to that love should become upward and outward—upward in worship, and outward in loving others. We've been forgiven a great debt, so we must demonstrate that forgiveness. We see this dynamic in play in Matthew 18:32-34, where a king has forgiven a man an impossible debt, only to find out the man nearly strangles someone over not paying an insignificant one.

> The king called in the man he had forgiven and said, "You
> evil servant! I forgave you that tremendous debt because
> you pleaded with me. Shouldn't you have mercy on your
> fellow servant, just as I had mercy on you?" Then the angry
> king sent the man to prison to be tortured until he had
> paid his entire debt.

We see the same debt language here. We've been released from a debt, so we must become a people who release debts—through the vehicle of love. The beautiful crux of Paul's words lies in Romans 8:10—that love does zero wrong to someone. If we love, we truly fulfill the law. This echoes what Jesus did. He loved with abandon while fulfilling the law. And his love did only good for those of us who have received it.

This upward and outward call of love is our mandate: Love God; love others. It's simple. Err on the side of love, my friend.

> *Father, I want to err on the side of love. Teach me what it means to love others with that kind of abandon—to graciously forgive even when I'm hurt, to consider it my holy obligation to love the people in my life, to give back what I've received from you. Convert my wallet as you create in me a heart that can't help but love others. Amen.*

Day 12

Read Romans 13:11-14

*This is all the more urgent, for you know how late it is; time
is running out. Wake up, for our salvation is nearer now than
when we first believed. The night is almost gone; the day of
salvation will soon be here. So remove your dark deeds like dirty
clothes, and put on the shining armor of right living.*

ROMANS 13:11-12

The progression of Paul's thoughts in Romans 13 is interesting—
from governance to love, and now urgency. Yes, we are to obey
the laws of the land. Yes, we are to love humanity. And now, in light of
all that, we are to wake up and be alert.

We can see this kind of dynamic today. As we look at governments,
wars, rumors of wars, poverty, and all sorts of hell on earth, we may
grow weary of it all. We could easily give in to a lackadaisical discour-
agement. Why do anything? The world marches on toward greater
degrees of sin and inhumanity. Why even try?

Because we are light bearers in a dark world. How we live matters.
We become good citizens so we can speak into the laws of our land. We
love the unlovely, demonstrating the fairness and love of the God who
pursues all people, not just the learned or powerful. And now? Paul
reminds us of the transitory nature of time—that, yes, it's marching
on, and our time is short. He uses words like *urgent, late, running out,
almost gone.* There's an immediacy to his words, a longing to rouse the
church to action.

And what is the action? Get rid of the old and put on the new. Run away from darkness toward the light. Shed sin and put on righteousness. All these are indications of our fidelity to our Father. We are people of day, of light, of right living. When we see sinful revelry, instead of gawking at its enticement, we expose it for what it is—an empty pursuit of hedonism. Because we have clothed ourselves with Christ, we cannot have fellowship with the darkness—it should repulse us. When we hear gossip and slander, it should (naturally) grieve us because this does not represent the kindhearted nature of Christ toward his people. Jealousy has no place in our hearts because we intrinsically understand the sovereignty of Christ over all. He holds our journeys in his hands, just as he holds others' journeys in his hands—no need to covet someone else's story.

Paul's encouragement follows a predictable morning pattern. We are to wake up, then put on clothes—wake up to the world careening around us (our time is short!) and clothe ourselves with Christ (who empowers us to make the most of our fleeting time).

> *Father, I look around me, and I get frustrated. Evil prevails. Wars. Pain. Death. Poverty. And I see the world spinning toward destruction. Instead of that making me stressed, would you awaken me to the tasks of the kingdom? I choose today to clothe myself with the righteousness of Christ. I need his compassion today, his empowerment. Amen.*

ROMANS 14

In the middle of this chapter, we see the
little phraseology of bowing before
God at the end of days.
I've created this as an anthem.

ANTHEM

Every knee will bend
Every tongue declare
That Jesus Christ
Is King

We are honored heirs
We will spend our lives
In allegiance
To his name

He was crucified
Resurrected, then
Interceding
For us now

He is seated high
With a glory crown
His Spirit indwelling
Us with praise

On another day
Jesus will return
And our tears
We'll shed no more

We will worship then
Justice rolling down
On heaven's
Pristine shore

Help us live right now
For the greater Then
Humbly serving you
Today

To remember you
Jesus, how you loved
When you showed us
How to live

Day 13

Read Romans 14:1-4

Accept other believers who are weak in faith, and don't argue with them about what they think is right or wrong. For instance, one person believes it's all right to eat anything. But another believer with a sensitive conscience will eat only vegetables. Those who feel free to eat anything must not look down on those who don't. And those who don't eat certain foods must not condemn those who do, for God has accepted them.

ROMANS 14:1-3

In this historical context, there were very real battles around the type of food people ate. In Acts, Peter has a vision that changes everything. He sees a sheet coming down from heaven. "It contained all kinds of four-footed animals, as well as reptiles and birds. Then a voice told him, 'Get up, Peter. Kill and eat.' 'Surely not, Lord!' Peter replied. 'I have never eaten anything impure or unclean.' The voice spoke to him a second time, 'Do not call anything impure that God has made clean'" (10:12-15 NIV).

Here God declares all foods clean, which must've been entirely perplexing to Peter—eat a reptile? Pork? Shrimp? But the crux of God's argument follows when Peter immediately receives an invitation to visit a Gentile, and he chooses to do so—another extreme *faux pas* for a Jew. There, in the home of Cornelius, he shares the gospel. The sheet-dream has informed and emboldened Peter, who says, "I now realize how true it is that God does not show favoritism but accepts from every nation the one who fears him and does what is right" (verses 34-35 NIV).

That's the heartbeat of this passage—that people are more important than food. The gospel is for all people, from all sorts of religious, non-religious, and dietary backgrounds. Mix Gentiles and Jews and former pagans together, and you get a stew of many beliefs—particularly about what is correct to eat to show your allegiance. Inevitably, there will be differences and preferences. What Paul is saying is this: Don't let your cultural or religious preferences cause you to prefer someone less. Love should rule our choices—right down to the food we put in our mouths.

Love those who cannot eat something. Love those who can. Respect those with differing food beliefs. You may think this has zero bearing on today, but as you scan food blogs, nutrition advice, and constantly changing doctrines about what is considered good and what is considered bad, remember that charity should prevail. No eating plan is perfect. But if we love, we are perfected.

> *Father, help me love everyone who loves you—even if they differ wildly from me. Give me a global view of the body of Christ. Empower me to love others in the way I view their choices. Instead of insisting on my own "rightness," teach me to walk around in the shoes of my friends and heap measures of love upon them. Amen.*

Day 14

Read Romans 14:5-9

*Some think one day is more holy than another day, while others
think every day is alike. You should each be fully convinced that
whichever day you choose is acceptable. Those who worship the
Lord on a special day do it to honor him.*

ROMANS 14:5-6

Paul shifts from addressing food rules to day rules—from *how* we
celebrate our relationship with God (via food) to *when* we feel it's
appropriate to celebrate God. This shows that how we live our lives
matters, but these external beliefs are not the summation of our Christianity. It's our heart before God and our love for others that trump
superficial rites.

More than the rules we place upon ourselves, Paul urges us to get to
the point where we are *fully convinced* of our beliefs. The Greek word
used is *plerophoreo,* which means to carry out fully, to be completely
convinced, to be persuaded. We see it a few more places in the New
Testament, and one other time in Romans, referring to Abraham: "He
was fully convinced that God is able to do whatever he promises" (4:21).

We become fully convinced of our beliefs by spending time with
God, watching his faithfulness over the course of our lives, reading stories of his power and redemption in the Bible, rubbing shoulders with
others who share our faith, and obeying him through the rough spots.
Like Abraham, the longer we walk with God, the more we believe he
is good and that he rewards those who seek him (see Hebrews 11:6).

Paul reminds us in this passage that our pet convictions should never sever someone from Christ. They're superfluous to the mission he has called us to—to live and die for Christ. Our allegiance should first be to Christ because he is our life. More than the body needs food, we need Jesus. More than experiencing the perfect day, we need Jesus.

If we live with Christ as Lord of our lives, all these worries about externals will pale in comparison to the joy of knowing him. We will be fully convinced of the most important doctrine known to man— that Christ died on our behalf in order to be the Lord of the living and the dead (Romans 14:9).

Father, help me love the people in my life who differ from me. Instead of pointing out the flaws of their beliefs, help me spend way more time becoming fully convinced of my own. And in that, I choose to follow you, the Lord of my life. You are the potter; I'm simply the clay, moldable in your hands. I trust you. Amen.

Day 15

Read Romans 14:10-13

Each of us will give a personal account to God. So let's stop condemning each other. Decide instead to live in such a way that you will not cause another believer to stumble and fall.

ROMANS 14:12-13

We know that God seeks after all people. The invitation throughout Romans is this cry of God that all will heed his wooing. So there is no place for elitism in the kingdom of God, nor human hierarchy. Why? Because at the foot of the cross, the ground remains level. We are all in need of a Savior, all desperately needy. None of us is righteous.

Since that is the case, it is ridiculous to condemn another Christ follower. How can we possibly know the workings of the human heart? And to look down is showing favoritism—it's saying you are better and greater than another. That's simply untrue. We are all laid low in our humble state. That's why Paul reminds us that we're in this adventure together as we bow before the One who saved us.

We see the language of kneeling throughout Scripture—usually in reference to human beings bowing before the majesty of God. The psalmist cries, "Come, let us worship and bow down. Let us kneel before the LORD our maker" (Psalm 95:6). Paul is quoting Isaiah 45:23 in Romans 14:11. It reads, "I have sworn by my own name; I have spoken the truth, and I will never go back on my word: Every knee will bend to me, and every tongue will declare allegiance to me." Paul revisits this idea in Philippians 2:10-11, saying, "At the name of Jesus every knee should bow, in heaven and on earth and under the earth, and every tongue declare that Jesus Christ is Lord, to the glory of God the Father."

When we marvel at the power and glory of God, it should so transform us that we can't help but kneel before him. Our reverence will inform not only our worship of God, but also our kindness toward others in the body of Christ. And we show them kindness by not causing their stumbling.

When we read Paul's writings about maturing believers, we learn they become more and more free. Freedom and joy typify someone who has spent time with Christ. But here in Romans Paul warns us that our freedom should never become an in-your-face proclamation over someone else being less-than. Our freedom, because of love, is constrained.

Father, I choose today to get on my knees before you. Worshipping you helps me understand my rightful place. It also reminds me that the cross is a level place, and I don't need to let my freedom hurt my fellow believers. Help me love others, not lord my beliefs over them. Give me your love to give to others. Amen.

Day 16

Read Romans 14:14-19

*The Kingdom of God is not a matter of what we eat or drink,
but of living a life of goodness and peace and joy in the Holy
Spirit. If you serve Christ with this attitude, you will please
God, and others will approve of you, too. So then, let us aim for
harmony in the church and try to build each other up.*

ROMANS 14:17-19

Paul speaks here of the temporary and the permanent. The temporary? Food. The permanent? People's souls. He's encouraging us not to ruin someone's soul for the sake of our own surface likes and desires—flaunting our freedom at the expense of the inexperienced. What should reign in our interactions with others is simply our love for one another. Think about what would bless that person, then joyfully choose to do it. Consider what would corrupt them, and graciously walk away from doing that.

Harmony in the church is utterly important. Jesus told the disciples this truth: "Now I am giving you a new commandment: Love each other. Just as I have loved you, you should love each other. Your love for one another will prove to the world that you are my disciples" (John 13:34-35). Our love proves our discipleship. Later, in John 17, Jesus fleshes out this idea in a prayer:

> I am praying not only for these disciples but also for all who
> will ever believe in me through their message. I pray that

they will all be one, just as you and I are one—as you are in me, Father, and I am in you. And may they be in us so that the world will believe you sent me. I have given them the glory you gave me, so they may be one as we are one. I am in them and you are in me. May they experience such perfect unity that the world will know that you sent me and that you love them as much as you love me (verses 20-23).

The degree to which we ardently love others is the degree to which we will accurately represent Jesus Christ.

Paul concludes today's passage from Romans by sharing that if we continue to increase in goodness, peace, and joy in our treatment of other people, we will not only experience the smile of God upon us, but we'll also experience the approval of others. Our aim, Paul asserts, is both pursuing unity and making every effort to build up our fellow believers.

Father, thank you for this reminder of the importance of unity. Not uniformity or robotic similarity, but unity of love. Help me serve those who are weaker in the faith than I am. Increase goodness, peace, and joy in my heart through the Holy Spirit. Show me someone today who needs encouragement. Amen.

Day 11

Read Romans 14:20-23

You may believe there's nothing wrong with what you are doing, but keep it between yourself and God. Blessed are those who don't feel guilty for doing something they have decided is right. But if you have doubts about whether or not you should eat something, you are sinning if you go ahead and do it. For you are not following your convictions. If you do anything you believe is not right, you are sinning.

ROMANS 14:22-23

Paul subtly reminds us of the power of the tongue. We boast of many things with our tongues—and we can also boast of our freedom in Christ so much that we alienate a newer believer. Instead of loudly proclaiming our personal convictions, it's best to stay quiet.

Such convictions aren't wrong. We build them throughout our lives as we interact with Jesus over the years. And sometimes those convictions change as we grow. We may not even agree with ourselves from ten years ago! And that's precisely why it's important to keep those to ourselves unless someone is sincerely asking why we do a particular practice or abstain from something. In the context of community, we can kindly explain why we've arrived at that conclusion, but even then, we must hold our conviction loosely, and we must continue to demonstrate grace and charity to someone who believes slightly differently.

This is not a call to throw away good doctrine. This is not Paul saying we should never talk about core beliefs. These food issues represent secondary issues of the faith.

Consider a target with a big red circle in its center. That center is the place where we as Christ followers unanimously agree: God made the world. He chose Israel to represent him to that world. Jesus is God's Son. He lived a sinless life, then gave his life as a ransom for us on the cross. He died and was buried. Three days later he rose from the dead, and someday he will return. These are our core beliefs.

We must discern the appropriate difference between peripheral issues (what we eat, where we worship, how we worship, and the like) and central issues (for example, whom we worship). In the former, we exercise restraint; in the latter, we hold to orthodoxy.

Father, thank you for reminding me about convictions that don't pertain to the centrality of faith. As I look back on my life, I see my own theology shifting, and I don't even agree with the me of a few years ago. Help me exercise grace with those who differ from me. Just as I give myself grace for seeing how my own beliefs have shifted with maturity, I choose to offer that grace to those younger in the faith today. Amen.

ROMANS 15

There's a time for every believer, whether they find themselves weak or strong, when they must understand the need for Jesus in their everyday life.

THE STORY

I've planted my dreams
In the heaviest soil
Spent much of my life
In a frenzying toil
Striving to prove my worth

My story, it ends
In frustrating destruction
Still I hear echoes
Of your great resurrection
Revealing your proven worth

CHORUS

Resurrect my life today
From the dust and miry clay
Sing your story over me
Jesus

I will sing about your fame
Death no longer shouts its
reign
Sing your story over me
Jesus

I've chased so many trinkets
Instead of your treasure
Tackled mountains and heights
The world cannot measure
Fighting to find my way

You beckon my trust
Past my strength's horizon
Woo me away
From a heart compromising
Giving a story, a song

BRIDGE

In the death of dreams, you
   find me
When ambitions cease, you
   find me
When my strength expires, you
   find me
At the end of myself, you find
   me
You sprout life from the grave, I
   praise you
You resurrect dying hope, I
   praise you
Your ways higher than mine, I
   praise you
You redeem every story, I
   praise you

Day 18

Read Romans 15:1-4

We who are strong must be considerate of those who are sensitive about things like this. We must not just please ourselves. We should help others do what is right and build them up in the Lord.

ROMANS 15:1-2

We must remember that when Paul wrote the book of Romans, there were no chapter breaks, nor was the letter neatly divided into verses. Here we very clearly see the continuation of thought from chapter 14, reminding us to be charitable with those who differ from us, to let love rule our hearts. This is the essence of servanthood.

Then (in Romans 15:3) he quotes from Psalm 69:9, which reads, "Passion for your house has consumed me, and the insults of those who insult you have fallen on me."

The first part of that verse is quoted in John 2:17 after Jesus cleansed the temple: "Then his disciples remembered this prophecy from the Scriptures: 'Passion for God's house will consume me.'" This reveals a bit about how deeply Jesus loves his people, particularly when they congregate. The church should not be a house of money laundering, but a place of peace and prayer. This meshes well with Paul's admonition of unity in Romans 14.

The second part, Paul quotes here in chapter 15: "The insults of those who insult you, O God, have fallen on me" (verse 3). Jesus took all the punishment for us. When we reviled God, he absorbed that sin. When we blatantly went astray, that betrayal pierced him. When he was tortured and crucified, instead of hollering, "It's not fair; I did nothing to deserve this treatment," Jesus stayed quiet. He obeyed his Father. He took the insults. In that way, he served both God the Father and all of us. And that example serves to inform the way we also should treat people.

Yes, you will be insulted. Yes, you will suffer for someone else's sin. Yes, this world will tear you to pieces. But take heart. Jesus has overcome all of this. He walked the path first so you wouldn't have to be alone. He bore the weight, and now bears you. And as he has taken on your burdens, he asks you to take on the burdens of others—to serve and build them up. A good teacher does that. He demonstrates how to do something, trains you, then hands you the keys.

Father, thank you for the reminder that you sent your Son to carry my sins, to receive the insults I hurled and the sins I committed upon himself. He bore the weight of it all, setting an example for me to follow in his steps. I want to do better at bearing the weight of others' stories and grief. Strengthen me, please, through the Holy Spirit within. Amen.

Day 19

Read Romans 15:5-6

May God, who gives this patience and encouragement, help you live in complete harmony with each other, as is fitting for followers of Christ Jesus.

ROMANS 15:5

Throughout Scripture we see God's emphasis on harmony. This doesn't mean there won't be discord in the church, but it *does* mean our aim should be to strive for understanding, choosing the other person's good over our will. You see this in play during the time of the kings. "God's hand was on the people in the land of Judah, giving them all one heart to obey the orders of the king and his officials, who were following the word of the LORD" (2 Chronicles 30:12). This principle of harmony, while it applies to close relationships, also informs nations and the way they succeed.

In the Psalms, we read, "How wonderful and pleasant it is when brothers live together in harmony!" (133:1). Have you ever had an experience where the opposite was true? It's hard to live life, to pursue the goals God has for you wholeheartedly, when you're mired in worry and sadness over a broken relationship. Having that unresolved conflict informs your day, shattering your resolve.

Paul reminds us in other epistles of this call to unity that Jesus put forth in the upper room discourse in John 17. Whereas prior to Jesus, Jews and Gentiles lived in hostility toward one another, now another law supersedes that belief—the law of love. "You are all children of God through faith in Christ Jesus. And all who have been united with Christ in baptism have put on Christ, like putting on new clothes. There is no longer Jew or Gentile, slave or free, male and female. For you are all one in Christ Jesus" (Galatians 3:26-28). Because we are all leveled at the foot of the cross and there are no more hierarchies, we don't need to claw our way to prominence. We don't need to malign another to promote ourselves.

Instead, we are to be gracious and forgiving—the new way of the kingdom. When we do this, as Paul reminds us in today's verses, we can, together, worship God. Worshipping him is our utmost duty and privilege, so laying aside our differences and taking second place is part of this grand worship. Paul instructs, "Make allowance for each other's faults, and forgive anyone who offends you. Remember, the Lord forgave you, so you must forgive others. Above all, clothe yourselves with love, which binds us all together in perfect harmony" (Colossians 3:13-14).

Jesus enabled this harmony by first offering himself so we could have peace with God. That radical forgiveness empowers us to forgive—and the act of forgiveness is the oxygen to the kingdom, giving us the ability to move beyond pain and differences to worship the One who made everything possible.

> *Father, I see now that harmony and unity are tenets of your heart. You long to see your children get along. Thank you for sending your Son to die for us all so that there is no longer a hierarchy in your kingdom. Lord, help me forgive those who have wronged me. Teach me humility. Thank you for extending so much grace my way so I can, in turn, extend it outward. Amen.*

Day 80

Read Romans 15:7-13

Accept each other just as Christ has accepted you so that God will be given glory. Remember that Christ came as a servant to the Jews to show that God is true to the promises he made to their ancestors. He also came so that the Gentiles might give glory to God for his mercies to them.

ROMANS 15:7-9

Paul continues his important discourse about Jews, Gentiles, and harmony by quoting widely from the Old Testament in today's passage (see Psalm 18:49; Deuteronomy 32:43; Psalm 117:1; Isaiah 11:10). He reveals to us that we cannot read the New Testament without the heritage and story of the Old Testament. In fact, throughout the book of Romans, Paul quotes generously from the only Bible he had, making an argument that God always had a longer story in mind for the reconciliation of all humankind.

His promises include the Gentiles. Yes, Israel was to be a light for the nations, but that light's purpose was to show God's glory and invite people to him. Israel's peculiarity (in the sense of that nation's people being chosen and special) was not meant for its glory, but for God's. He bestowed his favor so that the nations would long to know and worship him. But so often, Israel cherished its special relationship as a means to revel in its uniqueness. Or it enmeshed itself so much in the surrounding culture that it lost its distinctiveness as it followed after lesser gods.

So why does this matter? Because it reveals the longevity of God's plan and how beautifully God enacted it. Redemption of us all was his long-term plan, fulfilled by Jesus who came to earth not only for Israel, but also for the entirety of the human race. We're now God's ambassadors of hope for a world desperately in need of life, truth, and grace.

Paul concludes this history lesson with a prayer for you. He prays that God will give you this hope, that you'll experience joy as the truth of his choosing you sinks in. This radical choosing—inaugurated by the life, death, and resurrection of Christ—ushers in much-needed peace and utter confidence. You are his child. He moved heaven and earth to choose and save you in the grand narrative of Scripture. And now your response is to worship him and live joyfully empowered by the Holy Spirit.

> *Father, I'm humbled by all this. Thank you for showing me the overarching plan throughout Scripture—that you are constantly seeking the lost. Thank you for Jesus, who made a way for me to have peace with you, my Father. I love you. I'm grateful to be included in your narrative. I'm grateful to be chosen. Amen.*

Day 81

Read Romans 15:14-19

I am fully convinced, my dear brothers and sisters, that you are full of goodness. You know these things so well you can teach each other all about them. Even so, I have been bold enough to write about some of these points, knowing that all you need is this reminder. For by God's grace, I am a special messenger from Christ Jesus to you Gentiles. I bring you the Good News so that I might present you as an acceptable offering to God, made holy by the Holy Spirit.

ROMANS 15:14-16

Paul begins and ends today's passage with *fully*. He is fully convinced of the recipients' goodness—all the brothers and sisters who will be reading this letter. Since we've walked through many chapters of Romans that remind us we're all sinners and no good can be found in us, this is a curious statement.

Paul has, however, completed recounting the story of our redemption. Yes, we were sinners. Yes, we failed to pursue or acknowledge God. Yes, we were helpless to save ourselves from our sin nature—in fact, we were enslaved. But more yeses are in order: Yes, Jesus came to live the perfect life we could not live. Yes, Jesus died on the cross, taking upon himself the punishment for sin. Yes, he rose again, conquering death. Yes, we now have unfettered access to God; we are gloriously set free, beautifully redeemed. Now, because of the Spirit residing within us, we *are* full of goodness—to the glory of the One who brought it all about.

Paul ends by reminding us in verses 17-19 of the way he *fully* presented the Good News—through his humble service and the power of the Holy Spirit. He worked among those who needed to hear about God's plan. He didn't lord his authority over them, didn't come from a position of power, but served alongside. And in that service, he relied on the Holy Spirit. When he did so, miracles sprang forth. He didn't bring the miracles—the Holy Spirit did.

How Paul ministered is something we can learn from. Now that we've been made fully right with God, our task is to humbly serve those God has put on our pathway, trusting in the Holy Spirit to do the work. The miracles don't come through our might, but through his power. We serve others. We trust the Spirit. And the Spirit brings people to himself. That's the heart of Paul—to see others, Jew and Gentile alike, believe the Good News, becoming joy-filled ambassadors for the God who pursues.

Father, I'm grateful for the Good News—the news that transferred me from living for myself to living for you—fully alive, fully forgiven. Open my eyes to opportunities to serve others today. And empower me to rely on your Spirit to do the miraculous work—to bring people to you. I want to be part of your plan to see others meet and love you. Amen.

Day 82

Read Romans 15:20-22

*My ambition has always been to preach the
Good News where the name of Christ has never
been heard, rather than where a church has
already been started by someone else.*

ROMANS 15:20

This verse has had significant meaning to me, particularly as our family ventured overseas to plant churches. We wanted to go to a place where folks hadn't yet heard about Jesus. Coming from the Bible Belt in the southern United States and going to the south of France, where the predominant line of thought bent toward atheism, we learned a lot about contextualization of the gospel—and not from an American perspective. Perhaps that's one of the reasons Paul adopted this mind-set: When you share Christ with people of a different culture, you are able to see the gospel in all its power in an entirely different context. I doubt I'll ever get over hearing God worshipped in French.

In this passage, Paul refers back to Isaiah 52:15. Here it is in context (verses 13-15):

> See, my servant will prosper; he will be highly exalted. But many were amazed when they saw him. His face was so disfigured he seemed hardly human, and from his appearance, one would scarcely know he was a man. And he will startle many nations. Kings will stand speechless in his presence.

For they will see what they had not been told; they will
understand what they had not heard about.

This passage from Isaiah is referring to the Suffering Servant, whom
many Christian scholars believe to be Jesus. Paul, in using this reference, cements his view that Jesus is the fulfillment of this prophecy, and
that the gospel, which will now be preached to the ends of the earth, is
for all humanity, not a select few.

This prophecy points to both the supremacy of Christ and his sub-
sequent suffering on our behalf. Isaiah's words, and Paul's inclusion of
them in Romans, hint at the mystery of the hypostatic union—Jesus
is both fully God and fully man. Exalted, yet beaten. Prosperous, yet
impoverished. Isn't it amazing to see how Jesus continues to startle
many nations today? How he intersects all nations, all cultures, all people? What a privilege it is to serve him, to share his message of hope,
love, and justice with a world dying for all three.

There are microcosms of mission fields living outside your door.
You do not have to fly over an ocean to "preach the Good News where
the name of Christ has never been heard" (Romans 15:20). There are
neighbors, children, retired people, book club members, mechan-
ics, retailers, great-aunts, and gardeners who have managed to be
untouched by the Good News their entire lives. Today it's your privilege to present Jesus, the beautiful Suffering Servant, to those who desperately need hope.

*Father, thank you for the opportunity to share Jesus with
those who have yet to hear about him. I pray for open eyes
to see those folks today, as well as open hearts to receive your
amazing message. Thank you for sending your Son to suffer, die, and rise again, securing a place for me in your kingdom. He is Lord—Lord of my life, Lord of my choices, Lord
of my home. Amen.*

Day 83

Read Romans 15:23-29

*Before I come, I must go to Jerusalem to take a gift to the
believers there. For you see, the believers in Macedonia
and Achaia have eagerly taken up an offering for the poor
among the believers in Jerusalem. They were glad to do this
because they feel they owe a real debt to them. Since the
Gentiles received the spiritual blessings of the Good News
from the believers in Jerusalem, they feel the least they can
do in return is to help them financially. As soon as I have
delivered this money and completed this good deed of theirs,
I will come to see you on my way to Spain.*

ROMANS 15:25-28

Paul reveals his affection for the believers in Rome in today's passage. He painstakingly explains why he's been so long in visiting
them. He's been about the Lord's business, sharing Jesus with people all
over the known world—people who had never heard the Good News.

And now he's taken up an offering, a much-needed provision for
the impoverished believers in Jerusalem. We read about this offering
in 1 Corinthians 16:1-2: "Regarding your question about the money
being collected for God's people in Jerusalem. You should follow the
same procedure I gave to the churches in Galatia. On the first day of
each week, you should each put aside a portion of the money you have
earned. Don't wait until I get there and then try to collect it all at once."
(Read 2 Corinthians 9:1-10 to see how Paul carried out this promise.)

Carrying the generosity of faraway believers to Jerusalem ended up costing Paul his freedom—which, ironically, led to his later imprisonment in Rome. While he'd hoped to come to encourage the believers in Rome by a traditional way of travel, he instead is taken there by force—all for being a needed bridge between the Gentile and Jewish believers with their sometimes-acrimonious relationship.

We live in a world where we pragmatically believe in karma: If we are good, good things will happen to us. If we are bad, terrible consequences result. The kingdom of God is not karmic, however. Here Paul did something powerfully generous, and the aftermath did not go his way. This should encourage all of us who suffer for doing what is right. Isn't that the trajectory Jesus lived? He did everything right; he brought freedom and justice to the broken—and what happened? He was crucified. We can expect no less.

Father, help me when I suffer for doing what is right. I realize that I have deeper fellowship with you when I do, because Jesus walked that same route long before I did—and we have fellowship in the midst of turmoil. Instead of becoming discouraged, I pray you'd empower me to follow you all the more—with joy. Amen.

Day 84

Read Romans 15:30-33

Dear brothers and sisters, I urge you in the name of our Lord Jesus Christ to join in my struggle by praying to God for me. Do this because of your love for me, given to you by the Holy Spirit. Pray that I will be rescued from those in Judea who refuse to obey God. Pray also that the believers there will be willing to accept the donation I am taking to Jerusalem.

ROMANS 15:30-31

Paul shows his vulnerability here. You can almost hear hesitation as he nears Jerusalem with the Macedonian and Achaian offering. And his fear is founded—that's the place of his future arrest. But you also see how love trumps fear. He is more concerned that the believers in Jerusalem are relieved of their pain and poverty than he is worried for himself.

Paul models what gutsy faith is in this interchange. He doesn't deny his fear, tamp it down, grit his teeth, and move forward. No, he lets his friends know his worry, and he invites them to be part of a healthy solution—through prayer. Prayer, whether implicit or explicit, permeates all of Paul's writings. It is his oxygen, the way he loves those he shepherds, how he navigates the world. He understands the utmost power of prayer because he has experienced the omnipotence of God throughout his earthly journey.

We are no different. The Pauline model shows us how to live in this world—to be generous, share our fears, ask for prayer. His desire was to be with these believers, to experience mutual encouragement—something we lose in our online, not-in-real-life world. He also shows us how to endure trials in this passage—with joy, not resignation.

Paul also pronounces a blessing over the Roman believers, something that would change the way we live if we would choose to do something similar. Perhaps today is the day you say a blessing over a friend or write a blessing over another struggling believer—affirming God's nearness, kindness, availability, and love over them. Maybe today is the day you shed your fear long enough to pray for someone in person, in the moment. This letter Paul wrote to the Roman believers was his prayer—his heart on the page, a love letter to those who shared his heart. That's why he ends this section of his letter with blessing and hope.

We never do know the time or hour of our departure. We don't know what will happen tomorrow. But we can always be honest, ask for prayer, and pronounce blessing on those we love.

This paragraph is Paul's main conclusion of his letter. Tomorrow we'll delve into greetings and relationships. But what a powerful send-off! The peace of God given to all.

> *Father, thank you for the example of Paul here, who is vulnerable, yet doesn't hesitate to invite others into that vulnerability. Help me be like that. I want to become a person who isn't afraid to ask for prayer. I want to be someone who pronounces blessings upon others. Thank you for shepherding me through the book of Romans. May its many, many lessons sink into my heart and leak out through my actions. Amen.*

ROMANS 16

All these people Paul mentions in the last chapter of Romans are fulfilling their calling. I created this song as a tribute to the preciousness and tenderness of that calling. What a privilege it is to serve Jesus!

YOU ARE GOD

Fill my heart
So I can fulfill
Your calling, sweet to me
Resurrect my mind
So I can endure
The road beneath my feet

CHORUS

You are God
I am not
I dare not pull back in retreat
You are God
I am not
I live in awe of you who rescued me
You are God
I am not
Help me love them as you do
You are God
I am not
I surrender to your truth

Empower with love
My fickle heart
For the ones who walk away
Resurrect my grit
To persevere
For those needing your light

Day 85

Read Romans 16:1-5

I commend to you our sister Phoebe, who is a deacon in the church in Cenchrea. Welcome her in the Lord as one who is worthy of honor among God's people. Help her in whatever she needs, for she has been helpful to many, and especially to me.

ROMANS 16:1-2

It's easy to skim past the latter part of a New Testament letter, skipping over hard-to-pronounce names to get to the conclusion and move on. But there's gold in these farewells because they involve people. Paul commends actual human beings who walked this earth, who battled pain and weariness, who experienced moments of elation and gain. They are like us. And in this case, they offer an example for us to follow.

Paul entrusted this letter to Phoebe, a deaconess (a word that simply means a woman who serves the church). She would be his emissary, traveling notoriously dangerous routes, relying on the hospitality of Christians along the long journey, in order to bring these words of theology and encouragement to the Roman Christians. He doesn't call her *his* sister, but *our* sister, signifying that she belongs to the entire congregation. Paul also uses the word *prostatis* to describe the generosity of Phoebe—the only time he uses this term in any of his writings. The word simply means benefactress. Phoebe apparently had great means, but she freely gave it away. Like Lydia, Chloe, and Nympha, she financially supported the ministry of the church.

Paul met Priscilla and Aquila in Corinth (see Acts 18:1-3). They, like

Paul, were tentmakers by trade. This couple worked alongside Paul, and, according to this passage, risked their lives for him. It's inferred, too, that they poured out their lives for the Gentile churches. A year and a half after living in Corinth, Priscilla and Aquila accompanied Paul to Ephesus (see Acts 18:11,18-19), planting a church in their home. They were hospitable, theologically astute, and they loved Jesus.

Epenetus, a man whose name means "laudable" or "worthy of praise," was a pioneer believer. It shows much of Paul's heart of evangelism and discipleship that he greets this saint so personally and fondly. In fact, his affection for all these people should encourage us to pursue people with the same vigor, to open our hearts and lives to others.

Father, teach me through the lives of these people to love you more. I want to serve others. Enable me to be joyfully generous with the resources I have. Remind me today of my sisters and brothers around the world who love you. I want to practice hospitality like Priscilla and Aquila, serving others through my home. And keep me tenderhearted and open to those who don't yet know you. I want to be ready to share your message. Amen.

Day 86

Read Romans 16:6-13

Give my greetings to Mary, who has worked so hard for your benefit. Greet Andronicus and Junia, my fellow Jews, who were in prison with me. They are highly respected among the apostles and became followers of Christ before I did.

ROMANS 16:6-7

Relationships matter in the body of Christ. They are the sinew and strength of all of us. We grow best together, and although community can deeply wound us, relationships can also be agents of healing if we dare step back in.

Here we see the great "stepping in" of the apostle Paul. He has made relationships with at least 14 people listed in this passage, and he knows them both by name and character. He desires to specifically encourage each one. Imagine hearing your name read at the end of such a long letter! Yes, Paul values good theology and practice, but he also values the human beings God has strategically placed in his life.

We are to live in such a way that we could write this type of letter to the people whose lives have intersected ours. In this disconnected world where people move around and relationships shift and end, it is entirely countercultural, yet kingdom-inspired, to pursue the hearts of others. We do that by listening, by bearing people's stories, by praying for those in need, and by following the principles of Romans 12, where we associate with all types of people—particularly those who differ from us.

We show we're living like Paul when we love our enemies, welcome widows and orphans (people who cannot necessarily help us), and dare to engage when we'd rather retreat to the comforts of our homes and tailor-made media. People matter more than things. They are costlier than money, and their worth cannot be measured monetarily. Laughter around a table, stories shared openly with generosity—this is what makes up genuine life.

We often think of the apostle Paul as a staid theologian, church planter, and sometimes-angry preacher who calls people to account. While those things are true, this passage highlights his humanity, tenderness, and affection for the people for whom Christ died. If your ministry does not involve people, it is not ministry.

Father, thank you for this list of people—just ordinary folks following an extraordinary God, being faithful to the work you have called them to. I want to be like them. And I want to be like Paul. Pepper my life with people. Help me love them well, forgive freely, and pray often. I want my life to be full of relationships, and through them, I want to glorify you. Amen.

Day 81

Read Romans 16:14-16

Greet each other with a sacred kiss. All the churches
of Christ send you their greetings.
ROMANS 16:16

When Paul greets all these people, he uses the common Greek word *aspazomai,* which has more nuance than simply greeting others. It's a verb that also means to salute, welcome, or pay your respects to. This is an affectionate term, a word of endearment.

In this passage Paul greets ten more believers, both men and women, who are also part of churches. These churches are most likely communal, similar to the gathering of new believers in Acts 2:42-47:

> All the believers devoted themselves to the apostles' teaching, and to fellowship, and to sharing in meals (including the Lord's Supper), and to prayer. A deep sense of awe came over them all, and the apostles performed many miraculous signs and wonders. And all the believers met together in one place and shared everything they had. They sold their property and possessions and shared the money with those in need. They worshiped together at the Temple each day, met in homes for the Lord's Supper, and shared their meals with great joy and generosity—all the while praising God and enjoying the goodwill of all the people. And

each day the Lord added to their fellowship those who were being saved.

Churches in this era met in homes. They were bastions of light in a darkened world that hated Christians, so when people gathered, affection marked their interaction. They greeted one another with a holy kiss—something foreign to most Western audiences. To an Eastern audience, a kiss symbolizes deep friendship. We see this in the interaction with David and Saul's son Jonathan (see 1 Samuel 20:41 NASB). The absence of a kiss is mentioned by Jesus when he says to Simon, "You did not give me a kiss, but this woman, from the time I entered, has not stopped kissing my feet" (Luke 7:45 NIV). Also note that Paul uses the word *hagios* in Romans 16:16 to delineate the kind of kiss folks were supposed to give—a sacred one. In other words, don't greet one another with a lustful kiss, but a holy one, a kiss that symbolizes brotherly and sisterly love.

Paul ends verse 16 by reminding the Roman believers that, while they have affectionate fellowship with one another, they are not alone in the world. They're part of a dynamic whole—the church of Jesus around the known world. What a comfort that must've been to them!

Father, I want to have the kind of relationships that have godly affection at their center. Help me not only receive friendship from others, but also be a good friend. I pray for the church I attend—that we would experience this same kind of preferential affection. Thank you that I'm part of your larger body of believers all over the world. Amen.

Day 88

Read Romans 16:17-20

*Now I make one more appeal, my dear brothers and sisters.
Watch out for people who cause divisions and upset people's faith
by teaching things contrary to what you have been taught. Stay
away from them. Such people are not serving Christ our Lord;
they are serving their own personal interests. By smooth talk and
glowing words they deceive innocent people.*

ROMANS 16:17-18

We should always pay attention to the PS of Paul. He's said most everything he wants to communicate with the Roman believers, but it's almost as if he forgot one last thing and feels compelled to add it in here. Throughout the Pauline writings we see these kinds of warnings. One of those places is 2 Timothy 4:3-4: "A time is coming when people will no longer listen to sound and wholesome teaching. They will follow their own desires and will look for teachers who will tell them whatever their itching ears want to hear. They will reject the truth and chase after myths."

Paul's pastoral heart is to protect the flock entrusted to him. Jesus strongly cautioned the disciples about this danger Paul speaks of: "Beware of false prophets who come disguised as harmless sheep but are really vicious wolves. You can identify them by their fruit, that is, by the way they act. Can you pick grapes from thornbushes, or figs from thistles?" (Matthew 7:15-16).

Paul is also echoing his own warnings against wolves in sheep's clothing (recorded in Acts): "Guard yourselves and God's people. Feed and shepherd God's flock—his church, purchased with his own blood—over which the Holy Spirit has appointed you as leaders. I know that false teachers, like vicious wolves, will come in among you after I leave, not sparing the flock. Even some men from your own group will rise up and distort the truth in order to draw a following" (20:28-30).

Paul doesn't say to manage these types of wolves. No. He simply will not tolerate predators among the sheep because they cannot help but destroy a vulnerable flock. Instead, he warns the Romans of the poisonous nature of divisive people. They are to have *nothing* to do with them. Their love for the flock of God must supersede the "rights" of deceptive teachers.

It's important to remember, too, where these deceivers come from. Jesus said, "You are the children of your father the devil, and you love to do the evil things he does. He was a murderer from the beginning. He has always hated the truth, because there is no truth in him. When he lies, it is consistent with his character; for he is a liar and the father of lies" (John 8:44). No wonder Paul finishes this portion of warning with a nod to God's victory over Satan (Romans 16:20).

Father, help me be aware of people who bring division or teach contrary to what your beautiful gospel means. Give me discernment, please. And empower me to say no to those who would harm your flock. I want to be a shepherd who protects—all for your glory. Thank you that you have already overcome the lies of Satan. Thank you that you sent Jesus—Truth as a person—to combat all the deception in this world. Amen.

Day 89

Read Romans 16:21-24

I, Tertius, the one writing this letter for Paul, send my greetings, too, as one of the Lord's followers.

<small>ROMANS 16:22</small>

Does it surprise you to know that Paul actually didn't pen this letter? He used a scribe, an *amanuensis*—a common practice in his day where the person "writing" the letter dictated it to someone else, who then physically printed the words on papyrus.

Scribe Tertius's name is interesting as well—it means "third," and it was a common slave name. His was not the glorious up-front job—but oh, how important! Because of his diligent behind-the-scenes labor of love, we now hold the book of Romans in our hands.

Being a scribe was tedious and tiring—full of detail work and grammar. Tertius may not have received the glory for the theology inside the letter, but he did possess good penmanship, which enabled others to read the letter and benefit from it.

Even still, Paul reveals his own honesty by permitting Tertius to add his name to the letter, further showing us just how leveling the gospel is. Everyone plays their part (whether glorious or mundane) in the Body of Christ, as Paul reminded us in Romans 12. Contrast Tertius, possibly a slave, to Erastus, known as a city official (mentioned in Romans 16:23). The word Paul uses is *oikonomos,* which means a steward—a high-status political official from Corinth. Like Joseph in the book of Genesis, Erastus most likely managed a large household or government entity.

The gospel, Paul asserts in this last portion of Romans, is for all. For Timothy, his mentee and close confidant who traveled alongside him. For Lucius, Jason, and Sosipater, who met Christ through their Jewish roots. For Tertius, the scribe of unknown birth. For Gaius, who hosted a church in Corinth and most likely extended hospitality to Paul. For Erastus, who held a high office, and Quartus. All people from all strata of life. The gospel is the dynamic message that beckons poor and rich, weak and strong, mourning and triumphant, fretting and faithful, powerless and powerful, unknown and known.

How poetic that Paul continues his fidelity to the gospel even as he finishes this grand letter!

Father, thank you for choosing all kinds of people to do the work of your kingdom. Help me never think more of myself than I ought. Open my spiritual eyes to see the genuine worth of everyone in your body, no matter what their role or work. I'm grateful for the gospel—the beautiful message that welcomes all who dare come. Amen.

Day 90

Read Romans 16:25-27

Now all glory to God, who is able to make you strong, just as my Good News says. This message about Jesus Christ has revealed his plan for you Gentiles, a plan kept secret from the beginning of time.

ROMANS 16:25

Paul ends this powerful letter the same way he began it—emphasizing the Good News. He beautifully bookends the message to emphasize the letter's theme. Look at Romans 1:1-5 to discern the similarities.

> This letter is from Paul, a slave of Christ Jesus, chosen by God to be an apostle and sent out to preach his Good News. God promised this Good News long ago through his prophets in the holy Scriptures. The Good News is about his Son. In his earthly life he was born into King David's family line, and he was shown to be the Son of God when he was raised from the dead by the power of the Holy Spirit. He is Jesus Christ our Lord. Through Christ, God has given us the privilege and authority as apostles to tell Gentiles everywhere what God has done for them, so that they will believe and obey him, bringing glory to his name.

We see the Gentiles, God's redemptive plan, the glory of God, the Good News, the prophets' foretelling, Jesus Christ as the fulfillment of those prophecies, and proclamation.

In Romans, we see the overarching plan of God throughout the Bible, how he called a people unto himself, making them great—to be a light to all people everywhere. His goal all along was to bring all humanity to himself. Though Israel stumbled, worshipped idols, experienced exile, and eventually returned from exile, God used that very nation to usher in the New Covenant through Jesus Christ. Jesus fulfilled both the Law and the Prophets.

Jesus faithfully obeyed the law while perfectly fulfilling overt and obscure prophetic words. Because sin meant death, Jesus offered his sinless self as a once-for-all sacrifice for all humanity. While being reviled and mocked, he blessed those killing him with forgiveness, then died a pauper's death. His heart stopped beating. He had no breath. He lay silent in the grave.

Until Sunday. Resurrection flourished! Jesus lived! He lives today, having conquered death and sin forever. He will never die again, and he lives to intercede for you. This is the Good News Paul preaches—a grand narrative from Genesis to Revelation about God's seeking and saving those who are lost. And we are the grateful recipients of a grace unearned, a salvation beautifully gifted. What a poignant, true story—and God resides in the center of it all. This gospel, friends, can never be about us. It is always about him—which is why Paul ends this letter by giving glory to the only One worthy of it. Amen. So be it.

Father, thank you. How can I possibly thank you enough? I'm part of this unfolding story, which surprises and delights me. Thank you for saving me. Thank you for sacrificing your Son for me. Thank you for writing such a beautiful narrative. Thank you for your ever-expanding kingdom that pushes out darkness and ushers in glorious light. "Thank you" doesn't seem enough, but I love repeating my gratitude. Amen.

Notes

1. Brother Lawrence, *The Practice of the Presence of God the Best Rule of a Holy Life: Being Conversations and Letters of Nicholas Herman of Lorraine* (New York: Fleming H. Revell Company, 1895), 31.

2. Charles R. Swindoll, *Swindoll's New Testament Insights: Insights on Romans* (Grand Rapids, MI: Zondervan, 2010), 33.

3. "Romans 1:16-17 Commentary," *Precept Austin*, last modified May 11, 2017, accessed February 20, 2019, http://www.preceptaustin.org/romans_116-19.

4. "Romans 1:20-21 Commentary," *Precept Austin*, last modified January 26, 2017, accessed February 20, 2019, https://www.preceptaustin.org/romans_1.

5. "Romans 2:24-26 Commentary," *Precept Austin*, last modified June 16, 2017, accessed February 21, 2019, http://www.preceptaustin.org/romans_224-29.

6. Dietrich Bonhoeffer, *The Cost of Discipleship* (New York: Simon & Schuster, 1995), 44-45.

7. "G4102—pistis—Strong's Greek Lexicon (NLT)," *Blue Letter Bible*, accessed February 25, 2019, https://www.blueletterbible.org/lang/lexicon/lexicon.cfm?Strongs=G4102&t=NLT.

8. "Romans 5:10-11 Commentary," *Precept Austin*, last modified March 11, 2018, accessed February 26, 2019, http://www.preceptaustin.org/romans_510-11.

9. The NAS New Testament Greek Lexicon. https://www.biblestudytools.com/lexicons/greek/nas/katallasso.html.

10. "Romans 5:16-17 Commentary," *Precept Austin*, last modified February 21, 2015, accessed February 26, 2019, https://www.preceptaustin.org/romans_516-17.

11. The KJV New Testament Greek Lexicon, https://www.biblestudytools.com/lexicons/greek/kjv/basileuo.html.

12. Interlinear Bible, https://biblehub.com/interlinear/romans/6-15.htm.

13. "2288. thanatos—Strong's Greek Lexicon," *Bible Hub*, accessed February 26, 2019, http://biblehub.com/greek/2288.htm.

14. "3800. opsónion—Strong's Greek Lexicon," *Bible Hub*, accessed February 26, 2019, https://biblehub.com/greek/3800.htm.

15. Bob Deffinbaugh, "Everything You Ever Wanted to Know About Coveting—and a Whole Lot More! (Exodus 20:17)," *Bible.org*, May 13, 2004, accessed February 27, 2019, https://bible.org/seriespage/23-everything-you-ever-wanted-know-about-coveting-and-whole-lot-more-exodus-2017.

16. "Nothing is more often misdiagnosed than our homesickness for Heaven. We think that what we want is sex, drugs, alcohol, a new job, a raise, a doctorate, a spouse, a large-screen television, a new car, a cabin in the woods, a condo in Hawaii. What we really want is the person we were made for, Jesus, and the place we were made for, Heaven. Nothing less can satisfy us." From Randy Alcorn, *Heaven* (Wheaton, IL: Tyndale House, 2004), 160.

17. Rick Dunst, "Grapevine Rootstocks," *Double A Vineyards*, December 16, 2014, accessed March 1, 2019, https://doubleavineyards.com/news/2014/12/16/grapevine-rootstocks/.

18. "3466. mustérion—Strong's Greek Lexicon," *Bible Hub*, accessed March 1, 2019, https://biblehub.com/greek/3466.htm.

Acknowledgments

I would like to thank the apostle Paul for penning such a rich, theologically astute (and challenging) book!

Huge endorsement for Patrick DeMuth, with whom I have bantered throughout this book, idea upon idea. He's my favorite theologian and my constant friend. Sophie, Aidan, and Julia, my three intelligent adult children, I love you. May you each day understand more profoundly the mystery of God's grace.

Warm chocolate chip cookies should be in order for my Writing Prayer Circle, who has prayed for me for more than a decade—over each book! Gratitude goes to Kathi, Sandi, Holly, Renee, Caroline, Cheramy, Jeanne, D'Ann, Darren, Dorian, Erin, Helen, Katy G., Katy R., Anita, Diane, Cyndi, Leslie, Liz, Rebecca, Sarah, Tim, Tina, Nicole, Tosca, TJ, Patrick, Jody, Susan, Becky, Dena, Carol, Susie, Christy, Alice, Randy, Paul, Jan, Thomas, Judy, Aldyth, Sue, Brandilyn, Lisa, Richard, Michele, Yanci, Cristin, Roy, Michelle, Ocieanna, Denise, Heidi, Kristin, Sarah, Phyllis, Emilie, Lea Ann, Boz, Patricia, Anna, Kendra, Gina, Ralph, Sophie, Anna, Jodie, Hope, Ellen, Lacy, Tracy, Susie May, Becky, Paula, John, Julie, Dusty, Tabea, Jessica, Cheri, Shelley, Elaine, Ally, and Amy. This has been a particularly difficult year, so your prayers mean so much.

Thanks to David and Sarah Van Diest, agents and friends who have encouraged and empowered me—who live the grace message of Romans.

Thank you, Harvest House, for entrusting me with this important book. I'm grateful for Bob Hawkins Jr. and his encouragement. Thank you, Kathleen Kerr, for being amazing as always. Sherrie Slopianka, Jessica Ballestrazze, Christianne Debysingh, Betty Fletcher, and Ken Lorenz, thanks for being enthusiastic cheerleaders who are skilled at your work! Thanks, as always, Emily Weigel—I love what you've done with this series of covers.

About the Author

Mary DeMuth is a writer, speaker, and podcaster who loves to help people live re-storied lives. Author of more than 35 books, including Christian living titles, Southern fiction, and her latest devotionals, *Jesus Every Day* and *Healing Every Day*, Mary speaks around the country and the world. She is the wife of Patrick and the mom of three adult children. Find out more at MaryDeMuth.com.

Visit Mary at **MaryDeMuth.com**
and be prayed for every day at PrayEveryDay.show

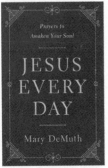

Jesus Every Day

Trying to juggle all your worries and burdens alone? Rediscover your compassionate Savior with this collection of daily heart-provoking prayers and accompanying Scriptures from author and speaker Mary DeMuth. Each reading will awaken your tired soul, prompt new ways to encounter Jesus, and inaugurate the kind of authentic conversation you've always yearned to have with Him.

Healing Every Day

In *Healing Every Day*, Mary DeMuth asks only that you show up, just as you are, hurting and broken and everything in between, to begin a 90-day journey of restoration through the Bible to a healthier, more whole you. This heartfelt devotional combines stories, Scripture, and prayers to reveal God's heart for the broken.

Seven Deadly Friendships

The friend breakup. It happens to everyone, but no one talks about it. Journey with Mary DeMuth as she guides you through the seven types of deadly friends, and discover the path to hope and healing through your ultimate friend—Jesus.

We Too

In the throes of the #MeToo movement, with authority and compassion, Mary DeMuth draws on her personal experience and elevates the voices of survivors as she unpacks the history of the church's response to sexual abuse in order to find a new way forward.